The Best-Dressed
Knitted Bears

The Best-Dressed

Knitted Bears

Dozens of Patterns for Teddy Bears, Bear Costumes and Accessories

Emma King

COLLINS & BROWN

This book is dedicated to my Nan

First published in the United Kingdom in 2009 by
Collins & Brown
10 Southcombe Street
London
W14 0RA

An imprint of Anova Books Company Ltd

ISBN 978-1-84340-490-3

A CIP catalogue for this book is available from the
British Library.

10 9 8 7 6 5 4 3 2 1

Reproduction by Rival Colour Ltd, UK
Printed by 1010 Printing International Ltd, China

This book can be ordered direct from the publisher.
Contact the marketing department, but try your
bookshop first.

www.anovabooks.com

Contents

Introduction

Whether it's tropical fun with Hula Bear, swashbuckling adventures with Pirate Bear or a magical time with Wizard Bear, *The Best-Dressed Knitted Bears* has a bear for every occasion.

I have had great fun creating this collection of knitted bears and their many outfits. Mixing traditional with contemporary styles I have designed a collection of six different bears ranging in size and complexity from a simple small-sized bear through to a large, more complicated bear.

The simple bear has minimum shaping and the body is knitted in one piece, as is the head. The intermediate bear has more shaping, the body is knitted in two pieces, and the head has sides and a gusset. The complex bear again has more shaping and also has the added interest of contrasting yarns and colours used to create the snout and the paws. There is also a jointed option for the complex bear. Each of these basic bears has a delightful wardrobe of outfits to choose from.

You can choose to knit the bears in the colours that I have selected, or you might want to personalise them by changing the colour or the yarn used. Information about alternative colours and yarns has been provided, so you can choose whether to knit your bear in a plain yarn or a tweed, or perhaps give your bear a touch of luxury by knitting it in silk or cashmere!

Why not knit a bear as a special gift? Golfer Bear would make an ideal present for any dad who loves to hit the links, and Safari Bear is perfect for the adventurers among us. These adorable bears are also a great way to mark an occasion – Newborn Baby Bear for a new arrival, Graduation Bear to celebrate the end of college, or First Birthday Bear for that important milestone. Or why not simply choose a bear to knit as a treat for yourself?

I have used colour, texture, sequins and many more techniques to bring the bears to life, and I hope you have as much fun knitting them as I had creating them.

emma king

Simple Small Bear

This little bear is easy to knit – you'll soon have a cute little friend to dress up as a princess, wizard or tooth fairy!

FINISHED SIZE
Height: 20cm (8in)
Diameter (around body): 16cm (6¼in)

MATERIALS
Option A (Beige)
- 115m (126yd) 4ply yarn. The bear on page 11 uses one ball Rowan Cotton Glace, 100% cotton, 50g (1oz), 115m (137yd), 730 Oyster

Option B (Cream)
- 115m (126yd) 4ply yarn. The bear on page 14 uses one ball Rowan Cotton Glace, 725 Ecru
- 3.25mm (size 3) needles (or size needed to obtain tension)
- 160m (175yd) 4ply yarn for facial features. The bear on page 11 uses a small amount of Rowan Calmer, 75% cotton, 25% acrylic, 50g (1oz), 160m (175yd), 481 Coffee Bean
- Large sewing needle
- 50g (1oz) toy stuffing

TENSION
23 stitches and 32 rows to 10cm (4in) using 3.25mm (size 3) needles and 4ply yarn, measured over stocking stitch.

BODY
Cast on 11 stitches.
Row 1: Purl.
Row 2: K1, (m1, k1) to end. *21 stitches*
Row 3: Purl.
Row 4: K2, m1, (k1, m1) to last 2 stitches, k2. *39 stitches*
Row 5: Purl.
Row 6: Knit.
Repeat rows 5 and 6 11 more times.

Row 29: Purl.
Row 30: K2tog, (k2, k2tog) to last 3 stitches, k3. *30 stitches*
Row 32: Purl.
Row 33: K2tog to end. *15 stitches*
Row 34: Purl.
Row 35: K1 (k2tog) to end. *8 stitches*
Do not cast off. Thread yarn through the remaining stitches and pull together to secure.

HEAD
Cast on 9 stitches.
Row 1: Purl.
Row 2: K1, (m1, k1) to end. *17 stitches*
Row 3: Purl.
Row 4: K1, (m1, k1) to end. *33 stitches*
Row 5: Purl.
Row 6: Knit.
Row 7: Purl.
Row 8: K2, (m1, k4) to last 3 stitches, m1, k3. *41 stitches*
Row 9: Purl.
Row 10: Knit.
Repeat rows 9 and 10 five more times.
Row 21: Purl.
Row 22: K1, (k2tog) to end. *21 stitches*
Row 23: Purl.
Row 24: Knit.
Row 25: Purl.
Row 26: K1, (k2tog) to end. *11 stitches*
Row 27: Purl.
Do not cast off. Thread yarn through the remaining stitches and pull together to secure.

LEGS (MAKE 2)
Cast on 8 stitches.
Row 1: Purl.
Row 2: K1, (m1, k1) to end. *15 stitches*

Row 3: Purl.
Row 4: K1, m1, (k3, m1) to last 2 stitches, k2. *20 stitches*
Row 5: Purl.
Row 6: K6, (k2tog) 4 times, k6. *16 stitches*
Row 7: Purl.
Row 8: Knit.
Repeat rows 7 and 8 nine more times.
Next row: Purl.
Next row: K2tog to end. *8 stitches*
Next row: Purl.
Do not cast off. Thread yarn through the remaining stitches and pull together to secure.

ARMS (MAKE 2)
Cast on 7 stitches.
Row 1: Purl.
Row 2: K1, (m1, k1) to end. *13 stitches*
Row 3: Purl.
Row 4: Knit.
Repeat rows 3 and 4 ten more times.
Next row: Purl.
Next row: K1, (k2tog) to end. *7 stitches*
Do not cast off. Thread yarn through the remaining stitches and pull together to secure.

EARS (MAKE 2)
Cast on 5 stitches.
Row 1: K1, p3, k1.
Row 2: K1, m1, k3, m1, k1. *7 stitches*
Row 3: K1, p5, k1.
Row 4: Knit.
Cast off, leaving a tail long enough to shape the ear and to attach it to the head.

FINISHING

HEAD, BODY, ARMS, LEGS

Each part of the bear has been knitted all in one piece, so will have only one seam. On the head and body, the seam will run from top to bottom down the centre back of the piece. With each piece, start joining the seams at the top and work two-thirds of the way down the piece, then use the opening to stuff the piece until it is firm (the body should be approximately 16cm (6¼in) in diameter). Sew up the remaining third of the seam. Fasten securely.

SHAPING THE NOSE

To create the snout, a running stitch is made, then pulled slightly to create a three-dimensional shape. Using the photo on page 11 as a guide, and working towards the lower section of the face, sew a length of yarn in a circular shape. When you are happy with the shape, fasten the yarn securely. If you don't get the right shape the first time, leave the 'wrong' circle of yarn threaded and use this as a guide to help you get a better shape. Pull the 'wrong' one out afterwards.

FACIAL FEATURES

Using the brown yarn (Rowan Calmer shade 481), sew the bear's facial features as follows:

Nose and mouth

The nose is an upside-down triangle. Using the photograph as a guide, mark where you want the nose to be.

Stitch the nose as follows: Insert the needle into the snout and take it horizontally under 2 stitches and then out. Now insert needle just below where it originally went in and, again, take it horizontally under 2 stitches, then out

just below the previous stitch. Continue in this way, ensuring you shorten each consecutive stitch so the nose tapers to a point.

Stitch the mouth as follows: With the same yarn, starting at the tip of the snout, sew a long single stitch roughly 1cm (⅜in) down and insert the needle into the head, then bring it out 0.75cm (¼in) to the left and slightly lower. Create a diagonal single stitch by inserting the needle back in through the base of the 1cm (⅜in) vertical stitch. Then bring the needle back out 0.75cm (¼in) to the right and slightly lower (opposite to last time) and create a second diagonal stitch by inserting the needle back in through the base of the 1cm (⅜in) vertical stitch. Take the needle down through the head and out through the underside. Fasten securely.

Eyes

Measure approximately 1.5cm (⅝in) up from the top of the nose and place a marker. Each eye will be positioned roughly 0.75cm (¼in) to either side of this marker. Stitch the eyes as follows: Leaving a long tail for securing, insert the needle into the right-hand side of where the eye will be, then, taking it horizontally to the left and under 1 stitch, bring the needle back out. Take the yarn back through once more in the same way. Then insert the needle into the original hole and, this time, take it down through the head and out through the underside. Return to the long thread you left at the beginning. Thread this onto your needle and insert it into the hole to the left of the eye. Take it down through the centre of the head and out through the underside. Pulling gently on these two yarns will set the eyes further into the bear's head, giving your bear's face character. When you have sewn both eyes, pull

gently on these yarns to create a face you are happy with. Then secure the yarns firmly to keep the features you have created.

EARS

Mark the position of the ears as follows: Measure 1.5cm (⅝in) to either side of centre seam; this is where the ear will start. There will be a 3cm (1¼in) gap between the ears. Using the long thread that you left when casting off, give the ear some shape by weaving the thread around the outer edge of the ear and then use the same thread to attach the ear to the head.

ASSEMBLING YOUR BEAR

Sew the head securely to the top centre of the body. Stitch the arms to the body at the shoulder approximately 2cm (¾in) down from the head. Sew the legs to the sides of the body, approximately 1cm (⅜in) up from the base of the torso.

Princess Bear

Little girls (and bigger girls too!) are certain to fall in love with Princess Bear. Her elegant dress and crown are finished with gorgeous beads and her soft mohair bodice is truly regal.

SKILL LEVEL
Intermediate

MATERIALS
For the dress and crown
- 115m (126yd) 4ply yarn (A). The bear's outfit opposite uses one ball Rowan Cotton Glace, 100% cotton, 50g (1oz), 115m (137yd), 828 Heather
- 210m (229yd) 4ply yarn used double throughout (B). The bear's outfit opposite uses one ball Rowan Kidsilk Haze, 70% super kid mohair, 30% silk, 25g (⅞oz), 210m (229yd), 579 Splendour

For the crown
- 175m (191yd) sock weight yarn (C). The bear's outfit opposite uses Rowan Shimmer, 60% cuprol, 40% polyester, ⅞oz (25g), 175m (191yd), 92 Silver
- 3.25mm (size 3) needles (or size needed to obtain tension)
- 500 approximately 3mm beads, such as Rowan 01014 in mauve
- Large sewing needle

TENSION
23 stitches and 32 rows to 10cm (4in) using 3.25mm (size 3) needles and 4ply yarn, measured over stocking stitch.

ABBREVIATIONS
PB Place bead: Bring the yarn forward, slip bead to front of the work, slip 1 stitch purlwise, take the yarn to the back of the work. The bead will now be sitting in front of the slipped stitch.
P2B Place two beads: Bring the yarn forward, slip two beads to the front of the work, slip 1 stitch purlwise, take the yarn to the back of the work. The beads will now be sitting in front of the slipped stitch.

DRESS
Skirt (make 2 for front and back)
Using 3.25mm (size 3) needles and A, cast on 19 stitches.
Row 1(WS): Purl.
Row 2: K1, (PB, k1) to end.
Row 3: Purl.
Row 4: K2, (PB, k1) to last 3 stitches, PB, k21.
Row 5: Purl.
Row 6: K1, (PB, k1) to end.
Row 7: Purl.
Row 8: K1, PB, (m1, k1, m1, PB) to last stitch, k1. *35 stitches*
Row 9: Purl.
Row 10: K1, PB, (k3, PB) to last stitch, k1.
Row 11: Purl.
Row 12: K1, PB, (k1, m1, k1, m1, k1, PB) to last stitch, k1. *51 stitches*
Row 13: Purl.
Row 14: K1, PB, (k5, PB) to last stitch, k1.
Row 15: Purl.
Repeat rows 14 and 15 16 more times, ending with a wrong-side row.
Cast off.

Bodice (make 2 for front and back)
With right side facing and using 3.25mm (size 3) needles and B, pick up and knit 18 stitches along the cast-on edge of one of the skirt sections, and work as follows:
Row 1: Purl.

Row 2: K3, m1, (k4, m1) to last 3 stitches, k3. *22 stitches*
Row 3: Purl.
Row 4: Knit.
Row 5: Purl.
Repeat rows 4 and 5 three more times, ending with a wrong-side row.
Row 12: K6, turn and work on these 6 stitches only as follows:
Row 13: Purl.
Row 14: Knit to last 3 stitches, k2tog, k1. *5 stitches*
Row 15: Purl.
Row 16: Knit to last 3 stitches, k2tog, k1. *4 stitches*
Row 17: Purl.
Do not cast off. Leave the shoulder stitches on a holder.
Rejoin yarn to remaining stitches, cast off centre 10 stitches and knit to end. Work on these 6 stitches only as follows:
Row 13: Purl.
Row 14: K1, k2togtbl, knit to end. *5 stitches*
Row 15: Purl.
Row 16: K1, k2togtbl, knit to end. *4 stitches*
Row 17: Purl.
Do not cast off. Leave the shoulder stitches on a holder.

Neckband
Join the right shoulder using the three-needle cast-off technique as described on page 26. With right side facing, using 3.25mm (size 3) needles and A, pick up and knit 6 stitches down the left front of the neck, 10 stitches across the centre front, 6 stitches up the right

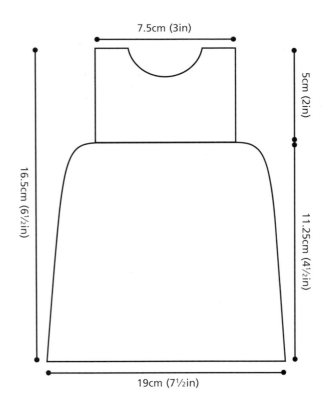

front of the neck, 6 stitches down the right back of the neck, 10 stitches across the centre back and 6 stitches up the left back of the neck. *44 stitches*
Cast off purlwise.

CROWN
Using 3.25mm (size 3) needles and A, cast on 19 stitches.
Row 1: K1, (p1, k1) to end.
Repeat this row once more.
Change to yarn C.
Repeat row 1 twice more.
Row 5: K1, P2B, (k3, P2B) to last stitch, k1.
Cast off.

FINISHING
Dress
Join the left shoulder using the three-needle cast-off technique as described on page 26. Join the side seams of the skirt section of the dress, leaving the side seams of the bodice section open.

Crown
Slip stitch together the side seams of the crown.

Wizard Bear

Conjure up some fun with this magical little bear. Complete with a hat, cape and wand, Wizard Bear will soon have everyone under his spell.

SKILL LEVEL
Intermediate

MATERIALS
For the cape and hat
- 175m (191yd) sock weight yarn. The bear's outfit on page 14 uses one ball Rowan 4ply Soft, 100% Merino wool, 50g (1oz), 175m (191yd), 383 Black
- Approximately 250 6mm sequins, such as Gutterman 1000 Black
- 10 silver star sequins in assorted sizes from 5mm to 14mm
- 3mm and 3.25mm (sizes 2 and 3) needles (or size needed to obtain tension)
- Large sewing needle

TENSION
28 stitches and 36 rows to 10cm (4in) using 3.25mm (size 3) needles and Rowan 4ply Soft measured over stocking stitch.

ABBREVIATION
PS Place Sequin: Bring the yarn forward, slip a sequin to the front of the work, slip 1 stitch purlwise, take the yarn to the back of the work. The sequin will now be sitting in front of the slipped stitch.

CAPE
Using 3.25mm (size 3) needles, cast on 47 stitches.
Row 1: K1, (PS, k1) to end.
Row 2: K1, purl to last stitch, k1.
Row 3: K2, (PS, k1) to last 3 stitches, PS, k2.
Row 4: K1, purl to last stitch, k1.
Row 5: K1, (PS, k1) to end.

Row 6: K1, purl to last st, k1.
Row 7: K2, (PS, k1) to last 3 stitches, PS, k2.
Row 8: K1, purl to last stitch, k1.
Row 9: K1, (PS, k1) to end.
Row 10: K1, purl to last stitch, k1.
Row 11: K2, (PS, k1) twice, k2togtbl, knit to last 8 stitches, k2tog, (k1, PS) twice, k2.
Row 12: K1, p5, p2tog, purl to last 8 stitches, p2togtbl, p5, k1.
Row 13: K1, PS, (k1, PS) twice, k2togtbl, knit to last 8 stitches, k2tog, PS (k1, PS) twice, k1.
Row 14: K1, p5, p2tog, purl to last 8 stitches, p2togtbl, p5, k1.
Row 15: K2, (PS, k1) twice, k2togtbl, knit to last 8 stitches, k2tog, (k1, PS) twice, k2.
Row 16: K1, p5, p2tog, purl to last 8 stitches, p2togtbl, p5, k1. *35 stitches*
Row 17: (K1, PS) three times, knit to last 6 stitches, (PS, k1) to end.
Row 18: K1, purl to last stitch, k1.
Row 19: K2, PS, k1, PS, knit to last 5 stitches, PS, k1, PS, k2.
Row 20: K1, purl to last stitch, k1.
Repeat rows 19 and 20 until work measures 13cm (5⅛ in) from cast-on edge, ending with a wrong-side row.
Next row: K2, (PS, k1) twice, k2togtbl, knit to last 8 stitches, k2tog, (k1, PS) twice, k2.
Next row: K1, p5, p2tog, purl to last 8 stitches, p2togtbl, p5, k1.
Next row: K1, PS (k1, PS) twice, k2togtbl, knit to last 8 stitches, k2tog, PS (k1, PS) twice, k1.
Next row: K1, p5, p2tog, p to last 8 stitches, p2togtbl, p5, k1.
Next row: K2, (PS, k1) to last 3 stitches, PS, k2.
Cast off.

HAT
Cone sections (make 3)
Using 3mm (size 2) needles, cast on 11 stitches.
Row 1: Knit.
Row 2: Purl.
Row 3: Knit.
Row 4: Purl.
Row 5: K1, k2togtbl, knit to last 3 stitches, k2tog, k1. *9 stitches*
Row 6: Purl.
Row 7: Knit.
Row 8: Purl.
Row 9: Knit.
Row 10: Purl.
Row 11: K1, k2togtbl, knit to last 3 stitches, k2tog, k1. *7 stitches*
Repeat rows 6 to 11 once more. *5 stitches*
Repeat rows 6 to 10 once more.
Next row: K1, sl2, k1, p2sso, k1. *3 stitches*
Next row: Purl.
Next row: Sl2, k1, p2sso.
Fasten off.
Join all three sections along side seams, leaving the last side seam open, and then work brim as follows:
Brim
Pick up and knit 28 stitches along the cast-on edge of the three joined cone sections.
Row 1 (WS): Knit.
Row 2: K4, (m1, k4) to end. *34 stitches*
Row 3: Knit.
Row 4: K1, m1, k10, m1, k12, m1, k10, m1, k1. *38 stitches*
Row 5: Knit.
Row 6: K1, m1, k12, m1, k12, m1, k12, m1, k1. *42 stitches*

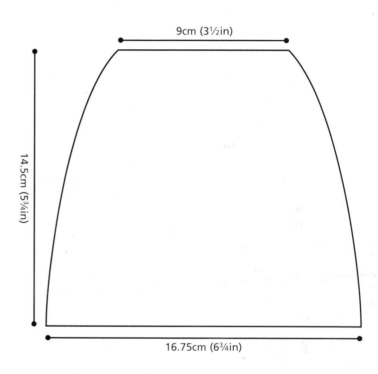

9cm (3½in)

14.5cm (5¾in)

16.75cm (6¾in)

Row 7: Knit.
Row 8: K1, m1, k14, m1, k12, m1, k14, m1, k1. *46 stitches*
Row 9: Knit.
Cast off.

FINISHING
CAPE
Make the tie at the front of cape as follows: Cut a length of yarn approximately 15cm (6in) long. Tie a knot at one end and thread on four or five of the different-sized star sequins. Stitch the other end of the yarn to the left front opening of the cape at the cast-off edge. Repeat for the right front opening of the cape.

HAT
Sew together the final seam of the hat by stitching from the edge of the brim all the way to the top of the cone.

Tooth Fairy Bear

This gorgeous bear just loves to help the Tooth Fairy. Put her under your pillow and her little drawstring pouch will be full of money by morning!

SKILL LEVEL
Intermediate

MATERIALS

For the dress, wings and pouch
- 115m (126yd) 4ply yarn (A). The bear's outfit opposite uses one ball Rowan Cotton Glace, 100% cotton, 50g (1¾oz), 115m (137yd), 831 Dawn Grey
- 210m (229yd) 4ply yarn, used double throughout (B). The bear's outfit opposite uses one ball Rowan Kidsilk Haze, 70% super kid mohair, 30% silk, 25g (⅞oz), 210m (229yd), 580 Grace
- 3mm and 3.25mm (sizes 2 and 3) needles (or size needed to obtain tension)
- Approximately 30 3mm clear beads, such as Rowan 01008
- Approximately 12cm (5in) white elastic
- Large sewing needle

TENSION
23 stitches and 32 rows to 10cm (4in) using 3.25mm (size 3) needles and 4ply yarn measured over stocking stitch.

ABBREVIATION
PB Place bead: Bring the yarn forward, slip bead to the front of the work, slip 1 stitch purlwise, take the yarn to the back of the work. The bead will now be sitting in front of the slipped stitch.

DRESS (MAKE 2 FOR FRONT AND BACK)
First frill section
Using 3.25mm (size 3) needles and B, cast on 81 stitches.
Change to yarn A.
Row 1: K1, *k2, lift the first of these 2 stitches over the second, repeat from * to end.
Row 2: (P2tog) to last stitch, p1. *21 stitches*
Row 3: Knit.
Row 4: Purl.
Repeat rows 3 and 4 twice more.
Break off yarn. Leave the stitches on a holder.

Second frill section
Using 3.25mm (size 3) needles and B, cast on 81 stitches.
Change to yarn A.
Row 1: K1, *k2, lift the first of these 2 stitches over the second, repeat from * to end.
Row 2: (P2tog) to last stitch, p1. *21 stitches*
Join the second frill section to the first frill section as follows:
With right sides facing, knit together the first stitch on the needle with the first stitch on the holder. Continue in this way until the whole row has been completed.
Next row: Purl.
Next row: Knit.
Next row: Purl.
Repeat the last 2 rows once more.
Break off yarn and leave these stitches on a holder.

Third frill section
Using 3.25mm (size 3) needles and B, cast on 81 stitches.
Change to yarn A.
Row 1: K1, *k2, lift the first of these 2 stitches over the second, repeat from * to end.
41 stitches
Row 2: (P2tog) to last stitch, p1. *21 stitches*
Join the third frill section to the second frill section as follows:
With right sides facing, knit together the first stitch on the needle with the first stitch on the holder. Continue in this way until the whole row has been completed.
Row 4: Purl.
Row 5: Knit.
Row 6: Purl.
Repeat the last 2 rows seven more times, ending with a wrong-side row.
Row 21: Knit.
Row 22: K1, p19, k1.
Row 23: K7, turn and work on these 7 stitches only as follows:
Row 24: K1, p5, k1.
Row 25: K1, k2togtbl, k1, k2tog, k1. *5 stitches*
Row 26: K1, p1, k1.
Row 27: K1, sl2, k1, p2sso, k1. *3 stitches*
Row 28: K1, p1, k1.
Row 29: Knit.
Row 30: K1, p1, k1.
Repeat the last 2 rows once more, ending with a wrong-side row.

Do not cast off. Break off yarn and leave the shoulder stitches on a holder.
With right side facing, rejoin yarn to remaining stitches and work as follows:
Row 23: Cast off centre 7 stitches, knit to end.
Row 24: K1, p5, k1.
Row 25: K1, k2togtbl, k1, k2tog, k1. *5 stitches*
Row 26: K1, p3, k1.
Row 27: K1, sl2, k1, p2sso, k1. *3 stitches*
Row 28: K1, p1, k1.
Row 29: Knit
Row 30: K1, p1, k1.
Repeat the last 2 rows once more, ending with a wrong-side row.
Do not cast off. Leave the shoulder stitches on a holder.

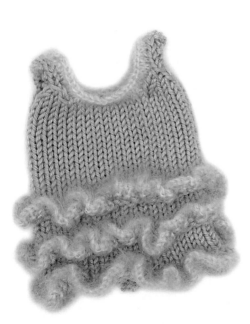

NECKBAND

Join the right shoulder using the three-needle cast-off technique as described on page 26. With right side facing, and using 3mm (size 2) needles and B, pick up and knit 10 stitches down the left front of the neck, 7 stitches across the centre front, 10 stitches up the right front of the neck, 10 stitches down the right back of the neck, 7 stitches across the centre back, and 10 stitches up the left back of the neck. *54 stitches*
Next row: Purl.
Cast off.

WINGS (MAKE 2)

Using 3mm (size 2) needles and A, cast on 5 stitches.
Row 1: Knit.
Row 2: K1, p3, k1.
Repeat rows 1 and 2 once more.
Row 5: K1, m1, knit to last stitch, m1, k1. *7 stitches*
Row 6: K1, p5, k1.
Row 7: K1, m1, PB, knit to last 2 stitches, PB, m1, k1. *9 stitches*
Row 8: K1, purl to last stitch, k1.
Repeat rows 7 and 8 until there are 25 stitches, ending with a wrong-side row.
Row 25: K1, (PB, k1) to end.
Row 26: Knit. (This creates the ridge for the turn-over at the edge of the wing.)
Row 27: Knit.
Row 28: K1, purl to last stitch, k1.
Row 29: K1, k2togtbl, knit to last 3 stitches, k2tog, k1. *23 stitches*
Repeat rows 28 and 29 until 5 stitches remain.
Row 48: K1, p3, k1.
Row 49: Knit.
Row 50: K1, p3, k1.
Cast off.

DRAWSTRING POUCH
Side (make 2)
Using 3.25mm (size 3) needles and B, cast on 25 stitches.
Row 1: K1, *k2, lift the first of these 2 stitches over the second, repeat from * to end. *13 stitches*
Row 2: (P2tog) to last stitch, p1. *7 stitches*
Change to yarn A.
Row 3: Knit.
Row 4: Purl.
Row 5: K1, yo, k2tog, k1, yo, k2tog, k1.
Row 6: Purl.
Row 7: K1, m1, knit to last stitch, m1, k1. *9 stitches*
Row 8: Purl.
Row 9: Knit.
Row 10: Purl.
Repeat rows 9 and 10 twice more, ending with a wrong-side row.
Do not cast off. Leave the stitches on a holder.

FINISHING
DRESS
Join the left shoulder using the three-needle cast-off technique as described on page 26.

Join the front and back sections of the dress as follows: leaving a 4cm (1⅝in) opening at the top of each seam for the armhole, join side seams.

WINGS

Each wing has a front and a back section which are separated by a garter stitch ridge. Fold along the garter stitch ridge so that your wing becomes double layered, and then slip stitch the side seams of the two layers together as neatly as possible. Repeat for the other wing. With the beaded side as the right side, stitch the narrowest edges of the two wings together.

Finally, sew a loop of elastic to each of the wings on either side of the centre seam. These loops can then be hooked over the bear's arms.

DRAWSTRING POUCH

Join the two bottom seams of the pouch using the three-needle cast-off technique as described on page 26.
Sew the side seams.
Cut two strands of yarn, approximately 40.5cm (16in) in length. Make twisted cord as described below:

Technique for making twisted cord:

Take the strands of yarn and secure at each end with knots. Ask someone to help you and give them one end of the yarn while you hold the other. With the yarn stretched out, twist each end in opposite directions until it shows signs of twisting back on itself. Bring the two ends of the cord together and hold tightly, allowing the two halves to twist together. Smooth out any bumps by running your fingers up and down the cord.

You will now have a twisted cord measuring approximately 16.5cm (6½in). If you would like a longer cord, start off with longer lengths.

Make a knot at each end of the cord, then thread the cord through eyelet holes near the frill and tie the ends together.

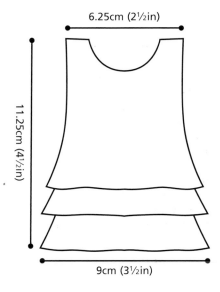

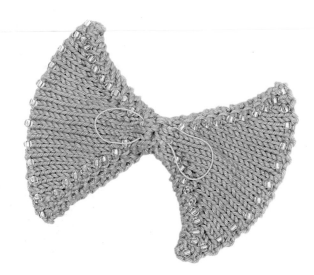

Simple Medium-Sized Bear

Dress this bear as a pirate, a ballerina or in a pretty springtime outfit – the choice is yours. Easy to knit and adorable in any colour, this bear is perfect as a gift or to keep for yourself.

FINISHED SIZE

Height: 27cm (10¾in)
Diameter (around body): 20cm (7¾in)

MATERIALS

Option A (Beige)

● 85m (93yd) DK weight yarn. The bear on page 28 uses one ball Rowan Handknit Cotton, 100% cotton, 50g (1oz), 85m (93yd), 205 Linen

Option B (Dark beige)

● 85m (93yd) DK weight yarn. The bear on page 22 uses one ball Rowan Handknit Cotton, 205 Tope
● 3.75mm (size 5) needles (or size needed to obtain tension)
● 160m (175yd) 4ply yarn for facial features. The bear on page 28 uses a small amount of Rowan Calmer, 75% cotton, 25% acrylic, 50g (1oz), 160m (175yd), 481 Coffee Bean
● Large sewing needle
● 50g (1¾oz) toy stuffing

TENSION

22 stitches and 29 rows to 10cm (4in) using 3.75mm (size 5) needles and DK weight yarn, measured over stocking stitch.

BODY

Cast on 11 stitches.
Row 1: Purl.
Row 2: K1, (m1, k1) to end. *21 stitches*
Row 3: Purl.
Row 4: K2, m1, (k1, m1) to last 2 stitches, k2. *39 stitches*
Row 5: Purl.

Row 6: Knit.
Repeat rows 5 and 6 11 more times.
Row 29: Purl.
Row 30: K2, k2tog, (k2, k2tog) to last 3 stitches, k3. *30 stitches*
Row 31: Purl.
Row 32: (K2tog) to end. *15 stitches*
Row 33: Purl.
Row 34: K1 (k2tog) to end. *8 stitches*
Do not cast off. Thread yarn through the remaining stitches and pull together to secure.

HEAD

Cast on 9 stitches.
Row 1: Purl.
Row 2: K1, (m1, k1) to end. *17 stitches*
Row 3: Purl.
Row 4: K1, (m1, k1) to end. *33 stitches*
Row 5: Purl.
Row 6: Knit.
Row 7: Purl.
Row 8: K2, (m1, k4) to last 3 stitches, m1, k3. *41 stitches*
Row 9: Purl.
Row 10: Knit.
Repeat rows 9 and 10 five more times.
Row 21: Purl.
Row 22: K1, (k2tog) to end. *21 stitches*
Row 23: Purl.
Row 24: Knit.
Row 25: Purl.
Row 26: K1, (k2tog) to end. *11 stitches*
Row 27: Purl.
Do not cast off. Thread yarn through the remaining stitches and pull together to secure.

LEGS (MAKE 2)

Cast on 8 stitches.
Row 1: Purl.
Row 2: K1, (m1, k1) to end. *15 stitches*
Row 3: Purl.
Row 4: K1, m1, (k3, m1) to last 2 stitches, k2. *20 stitches*
Row 5: Purl.
Row 6: K6, (k2tog) 4 times, k6. *16 stitches*
Row 7: Purl.
Row 8: Knit.
Repeat rows 7 and 8 nine more times.
Next row: Purl.
Next row: (K2tog) to end. *8 stitches*
Next row: Purl.
Do not cast off. Thread yarn through the remaining stitches and pull together to secure.

ARMS (MAKE 2)

Cast on 7 stitches.
Row 1: Purl.
Row 2: K1, (m1, k1) to end. *13 stitches*
Row 3: Purl.
Row 4: Knit.
Repeat rows 3 and 4 10 more times.
Next row: Purl.
Next row: K1, (k2tog) to end. *7 stitches*
Do not cast off. Thread yarn through the remaining stitches and pull together to secure.

EARS (MAKE 2)

Cast on 5 stitches.
Row 1: K1, p3, k1.
Row 2: K1, m1, k3, m1, k1. *7 stitches*
Row 3: K1, p5, k1.
Row 4: Knit.

Cast off, leaving a long enough thread to shape the ear and attach it to the head.

FINISHING
HEAD, BODY, ARMS, LEGS
Each part of the bear has been knitted all in one piece, so will have only one seam. On the head and body, the seam will run from top to bottom down the centre back of the piece. With each piece, start joining the seams at the top and work two-thirds of the way down the piece, then use the opening to stuff the piece until it is firm (the body should be approximately 20cm (7¾in) in diameter). Sew up the remaining third of the seam. Fasten securely.

SHAPING THE NOSE
To create the snout, a running stitch is made, then pulled slightly to create a three-dimensional shape. Using the photograph on page 22 as a guide, and working towards the lower section of the face, sew a length of yarn in a circular shape. When you are happy with the shape, fasten the yarn securely. If you don't get the right shape the first time, leave the 'wrong' circle of yarn threaded, and use this as a guide to help you get a better shape. Pull the 'wrong' one out afterwards.

FACIAL FEATURES
Using the brown yarn (Rowan Calmer shade 481), sew the bear's facial features as follows:

Nose and mouth
The nose is an upside-down triangle. Using the photograph as a guide, mark where you want the nose to be.

Stitch the nose as follows: Insert the needle into the snout and take it horizontally under 3 stitches and then out. Now insert needle just

below where it originally went in and, again, take it horizontally under 3 stitches, then out just below the previous stitch. Continue in this way, ensuring you shorten each consecutive stitch so the nose tapers to a point.

Stitch the mouth as follows: With the same yarn, starting at the tip of the snout, sew a long single stitch roughly 1.25cm (½in) down and insert the needle into the head, then bring it out 0.75cm (¼in) to the left and slightly lower. Create a diagonal single stitch by inserting the needle back in through the base of the 1.25cm (½in) vertical stitch. Then bring the needle back out 0.75cm (¼in) to the right and slightly lower (opposite to last time) and create a second diagonal stitch by inserting the needle back in through the base of the 1.25cm (½in) vertical stitch. Take the needle down through the head and out through the underside. Fasten securely.

Eyes
Measure approximately 2cm (¾in) up from the top of the nose and place a marker. Each eye will be positioned roughly 1.5cm (⅝in) to either side of this marker. Stitch the eyes as follows: Leaving a long tail for securing, insert the needle into the right-hand side of where the eye will be, then, taking it horizontally to the left and under 1 stitch, bring the needle back out. Take the yarn back through once more in the same way. Then insert the needle into the original hole and, this time, take it down through the head and out through the underside. Return to the long thread you left at the beginning. Thread this onto your needle and insert it into the hole to the left of the eye. Take it down through the centre of the head and out through the underside. Pulling gently on these two yarns will set the eyes further into the bear's head, giving your bear's face

character. When you have sewn both eyes, pull gently on these yarns to create a face you are happy with. Then secure the yarns firmly to keep the features you have created.

EARS
Mark the position of the ears as follows: Measure 1.75cm (⅝in) either side of centre seam – this is where the ear will start. There will be a 3.5cm (1⅜in) gap between the ears. Using the long thread that you left when casting off, give the ear some shape by weaving the thread around the outer edge of the ear and then use the same thread to attach the ear to the head.

ASSEMBLING YOUR BEAR
Sew the head securely to the top centre of the body. Stitch the arms to the body at the shoulder approximately 3cm (1¼in) down from the head. Sew the legs to the sides of the body, approximately 1.5cm (⅝in) from the base of the torso.

Pirate Bear

Ready to sail the seven seas, Pirate Bear is sure to be a hit with adventurers young and old. His ruffled shirt, pirate hat and sword give him a real swashbuckling look.

SKILL LEVEL
Intermediate

MATERIALS
For the trousers
- 113m (123yd) DK weight yarn (A). The bear's outfit opposite uses one ball Rowan Scottish Tweed DK, 100% wool, 50g (1oz), 130m (142yd), 023 Midnight

For the shirt
- 115m (126yd) 4ply yarn (B). The bear's outfit opposite uses one ball Rowan Cotton Glace, 100% cotton, 50g (1oz), 115m (137yd), 726 Bleached

For the belt, hat and sword handle
- 115m (126yd) 4ply yarn (C). The bear's outfit opposite uses one ball Rowan Cotton Glace, 727 Black

For the sash
- 160m (175yd) 4ply yarn (D). The bear's outfit opposite uses one ball Rowan Calmer, 75% cotton, 25% acrylic, 50g (1oz), 160m (175yd), 492 Garnet

For the sword
- 175m (191yd) sock weight yarn (E). The bear's outfit opposite uses a small amount of Rowan Shimmer, 60% cuprol, 40% polyester, 25g (⁷⁄₈oz), 175m (191yd), 92 Silver
- 2cm (¾in) buckle
- 3.25mm and 4mm (sizes 3 and 6) needles (or size needed to obtain tension)
- 3mm (size 2) double-pointed needles (or size needed to obtain tension)
- Large sewing needle

TENSION
TROUSERS
22 stitches and 30 rows to 10cm (4in) using 4mm (size 6) needles and DK weight yarn, measured over stocking stitch.

SHIRT
23 stitches and 32 rows to 10cm (4in) using 3.25mm (size 3) needles and 4ply yarn, measured over stocking stitch.

WAISTCOAT
25 stitches and 34 rows to 10cm (4in) using 4mm (size 6) needles and 4ply yarn, measured over stocking stitch.

TROUSERS

Front

Leg (make 2)

Using 4mm (size 6) needles and A, cast on 7 stitches.

Row 1: Purl.
Row 2: K1, (m1, k1) to end. *13 stitches*
Row 3: Purl.
Row 4: K1, k2, m1, (k3, m1) to end. *17 stitches*
Row 5: Purl.
Row 6: Knit.
Row 7: Purl.

Repeat rows 6 and 7 seven more times, ending with a wrong-side row.

Do not cast off. Leave the stitches on a holder. Join the two legs of the front as follows: With right sides facing, knit across 16 stitches of the left leg, knit the last stitch of the left leg together with the first stitch of the right leg, knit to end. *33 stitches*

Next row: Purl.
Next row: K2, k2tog, (k1, k2tog) to last 2 stitches, k2. *23 stitches*
Next row: Purl.
Next row: Knit.

Next row: Purl.
Repeat the last 2 rows four more times. Cast off.

Back

Work as for the Front.

SHIRT

Back

Using 3.25mm (size 3) needles and B, cast on 29 stitches.

Row 1: Knit.
Row 2: Purl.

Repeat rows 1 and 2 13 more times, ending with a wrong-side row.

Next row: K8, cast off centre 13 stitches, k8.

Do not cast off. Leave the two sets of shoulder stitches on a holder.

Front

Using 3.25mm (size 3) needles and B, cast on 29 stitches.

Row 1: Knit.
Row 2: Purl.

Repeat rows 1 and 2 nine more times, ending with a wrong-side row.

Row 21: K12, turn and work on these stitches only as follows:
Row 22: K1, purl to end.
Row 23: Knit to last 3 stitches, k2tog, k1. *11 stitches*
Row 24: K1, purl to end.
Row 25: Knit to last 3 stitches, k2tog, k1. *10 stitches*
Repeat rows 24 and 25 twice more. *8 stitches*
Row 30: K1, purl to end.

Do not cast off. Leave the shoulder stitches on a holder.

With right side facing, rejoin the yarn to the remaining stitches and work as follows:

Next row: Cast off centre 5 stitches, knit to end. *12 stitches*

Next row: Purl to last stitch, k1.
Next row: K1, k2togtbl, knit to end. *11 stitches*
Next row: Purl to last stitch, k1.
Next row: K1, k2togtbl, knit to end. *10 stitches*
Repeat the last 2 rows twice more. *8 stitches*
Next row: Purl to last stitch, k1.

Do not cast off. Leave the shoulder stitches on a holder.

SLEEVES (MAKE 2)

Using 3.25mm (size 3) needles and B, cast on 73 stitches

Row 1: K1, *k2, lift first of these 2 stitches over second, repeat from * to end. *37 stitches*
Row 2: (P2tog) to last stitch, p1. *19 stitches*
Row 3: Knit.
Row 4: Purl.
Row 5: K1, (m1, k1) to end. *37 stitches*
Row 6: Purl.
Row 7: Knit.

Repeat rows 6 and 7 four more times, ending with a right-side row.

Next row: P1, (p2tog) to end. *19 stitches*
Cast off.

FRILL COLLAR

Using 3.25mm (size 3) needles and B, cast on 93 stitches.

Row 1: K1, *k2, lift first of these 2 stitches over second, repeat from * to end. *47 stitches*

Row 2: (P2tog) to last stitch, p1. *24 stitches*

Cast off.

WAISTCOAT

Left front

Using 4mm (size 6) needles and D, cast on 7 stitches.

Row 1: Knit.

Row 2: K1, p5, k1.

Repeat rows 1 and 2 twice more, ending with a wrong-side row.

Row 7: K1, m1, knit to end. *8 stitches*

Row 8: K1, purl to last stitch, k1.

Row 9: Knit.

Row 10: K1, purl to last stitch, k1.

Row 11: K1, m1, knit to end. *9 stitches*

Repeat rows 8 to 11 twice more. *11 stitches*

*Row 20: K1, p9, k1.

Row 21: Knit.

Row 22: K1, p9, k1.

Repeat rows 21 and 22 four more times, ending with a wrong-side row.

Row 31: K1, k2togtbl, knit to last 3 stitches, k2tog, k1. *9 stitches*

Row 32: K1, p9, k1.

Row 33: K1, k2togtbl, knit to last 3 stitches, k2tog, k1. *7 stitches*

Repeat rows 32 and 33 once more. *5 stitches*

Row 36: K1, p3, k1.

Row 37: K1, sl2, k1, p2sso, k1. *3 stitches*

Row 38: K1, p1, k1.

Row 39: K3tog.

Fasten off.

Right front

Using 4mm (size 6) needles and D, cast on 7 stitches.

Row 1: Knit.

Row 2: K1, p5, k1.

Repeat rows 1 and 2 twice more, ending with a wrong-side row.

Row 7: Knit to last stitch, m1, k1. *8 stitches*

Row 8: K1, purl to last stitch, k1.

Row 9: Knit.

Row 10: K1, purl to last stitch, k1.

Row 11: K to last stitch, m1, k1. *9 stitches*

Repeat rows 8 to 11 twice more. *11 stitches*

Work as for left front from * to end.

Back

With right side facing and using 4mm (size 6) needles and D, pick up and knit 7 stitches along the cast-on edge of the left front, turn, and cast on 11 stitches, turn, and pick up and knit 7 stitches along the cast-on edge of the right front. *25 stitches*

Row 1: K1, purl to last stitch, k1.

Row 2: Knit.

Repeat rows 1 and 2 13 more times, ending with a right-side row.

Row 29: K1, p23, k1.

Row 30: K1, k2togtbl, knit to last 3 stitches, k2tog, k1. *23 stitches*

Row 31: K1, p2tog, purl to last 3 stitches, p2togtbl, k1. *21 stitches*

Repeat rows 30 and 31 until 5 stitches remain.

Row 40: K1, sl2, k1, p2sso, k1. *3 stitches*

Next row: P3tog.

Fasten off.

BELT

Using 3.25mm (size 3) needles and C, cast on 5 stitches.

Row 1: Knit.

Row 2: K1, p1, k1.

Repeat rows 1 and 2 until belt measures 29cm (11⅝in) from cast-on edge.

Cast off.

HAT

Peak

Using 3.25mm (size 3) needles and C, cast on 5 stitches.

Row 1: K1, (m1, k1) to end. *9 stitches*

Row 2: Purl.

Row 3: K1, (m1, k1) to end. *17 stitches*

Repeat rows 2 and 3 one more time. *33 stitches*

Row 6: Purl.

Row 7: Knit.

Row 8: Purl.

Repeat rows 7 and 8 once more, ending with a wrong-side row.

Cast off.

SASH

Using 3.25mm (size 3) needles and D, cast on 4 stitches.

Row 1: Knit.
Row 2: K1, p2, k1.

Repeat rows 1 and 2 until sash measures 26cm (10¼in) from cast-on edge.
Cast off.

SWORD

Blade

Using the technique described below, make the sword blade out of an I-cord as follows:
Using 3mm (size 2) double-pointed needles and E, cast on 5 stitches.

Row 1: Knit.

Repeat this row until cord is 4cm (1⅝in) long.

Next row: K2tog, k1, k2tog.
Next row: Knit.
Next row: K3tog.

Fasten off.

Technique for making I-cord: Once you have cast on your stitches, you must knit 1 row. You would now usually turn your needles, but to make the cord, do not turn. Instead, slide the stitches to the other end of the double-pointed needle ready to be knitted again. The yarn will now be at the left edge of the knitting and so to knit, you must pull it tightly across the back of your work and then knit 1 row. You continue in this way, never turning, and always sliding the work to the other end of the double-pointed needle. The right side of the work will always be facing you.

SWORD HANDLE

Using 3.25mm (size 3) needles and C, cast on 14 stitches.

Row 1: Knit.
Row 2: (P2tog) to end.
7 stitches
Row 3: Knit.
Row 4: Purl.

Cast off.

FINISHING

TROUSERS

Join the front and back of the trousers as follows: Sew the outer side seams. Start at the top (the cast-off edge) and work down to the bottom (the cast-on edge). Now, join the inner leg seams starting at the cast-on edge of the right leg, working up to the top, and then working down the corresponding seam of the left leg.

SHIRT

Slip the right front shoulder stitches and the right back shoulder stitches onto needles. Join the right shoulder seam using the three-needle cast-off technique given below, then repeat for the left shoulder seam.

Three needle cast-off: This technique allows you to join two pieces of knitting by casting them off together instead of sewing them together. The method is worked by placing the two pieces of knitting (each piece on a needle) together in the left hand with right sides facing each other. With a third needle, cast off the two rows of stitches together. Insert the right needle through the stitch on the front needle and through the stitch on the back needle and work them together. Repeat and cast off in the usual way.

Collar

Stitch the cast-off edge of the frill collar to the front neck edge starting at one shoulder, working down the front neck, across the centre neck and then up the other side of the neck.

Sleeves

Fold the sleeve in half lengthwise and mark the centre of the cast-off edge with a stitch marker. Line up this marker with the shoulder seam and baste the sleeve in place, then sew the sleeve to the body. Attach both sleeves in the same way.
Join both side and sleeve seams.

WAISTCOAT

Sew side seams, leaving 5cm (2in) open near the shoulder edges for armholes.

HAT

Join the peak to the sash as follows:
Measure approximately 4cm (1⅝in) from the cast-on edge of the sash, along the side seam. Place a marker. Starting at the marker, stitch the bottom edge of the peak (the side seams and the original 5 cast-on stitches) to the side of the sash. There should then be approximately 13cm (5⅛in) of sash remaining. Using the photograph as a guide, coil the sash around and sew the cast-off edge of the sash to the wrong-side side of the sash at the point where the marker is.

BELT

Thread the buckle onto one end of the belt.

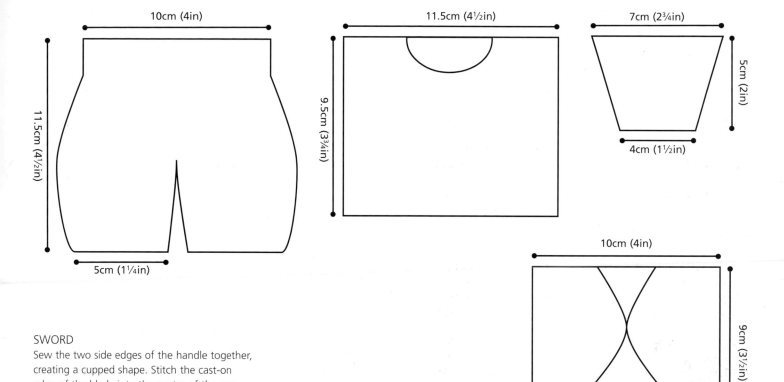

10cm (4in)

11.5cm (4½in)

5cm (1¼in)

11.5cm (4½in)

9.5cm (3¾in)

7cm (2¾in)

5cm (2in)

4cm (1½in)

10cm (4in)

9cm (3½in)

SWORD
Sew the two side edges of the handle together, creating a cupped shape. Stitch the cast-on edge of the blade into the centre of the cup and secure. Thread a loop of yarn through the handle so that the sword can be carried by the bear if desired.

SKILL LEVEL
Intermediate

MATERIALS
For the skirt, cardigan and ballet slippers
- 160m (175yd) 4ply yarn (A). The oufit for the bear on this page uses one ball Rowan Calmer, 75% cotton, 25% acrylic, 50g (1oz), 113m (124yd), 488 Sugar
- 210m (229yd) 4ply yarn (B). The outfit for the bear on this page uses one ball Rowan Kidsilk Haze, 70% super kid mohair, 30% silk, 25g (7/8oz), 210m (229yd), 634 Cream
- 4mm (size 6) needles (or size needed to obtain tension)
- Approximately 170 6mm iridescent sequins, such as Gutterman 1050
- Approximately 70cm (27½in) of 3mm (1/8in)-wide cream ribbon
- Large sewing needle

TENSION
25 stitches and 34 rows to 10cm (4in) using 4mm (size 6) needles and 4ply yarn, measured over stocking stitch.

ABBREVIATION
ML Place sequin on a loop. Knit into the next stitch and, before slipping the stitch off the left needle, slide a sequin up to the needle and bring the yarn to the front of the work between the needle points. Wrap the yarn around your left thumb and take it back between the needle points. Now, knit into the stitch again and then slip the stitch off the needle. You will now have

Ballerina Bear

Pretty in pink, Ballerina Bear is ready and waiting to dance for you. Her gorgeous ballet shoes are laced with ribbons and her tutu is covered with beautiful sequins to catch the light as she twirls.

two stitches on the right-hand needle. Cast one off by lifting one stitch over the other.

SKIRT
Using 4mm (size 6) needles and A, cast on 51 stitches.
Row 1: K1, (p1, k1) to end.
Row 2: Repeat row 1.
Row 3: Knit.
Row 4: Purl.
Row 5: K3, (m1, k5) to last 3 stitches, m1, k3.
61 stitches
Row 6: Purl.
Row 7: K1, (ML, k1) to end.
Row 8: Purl.
Row 9: K2, (ML, k1) to last 3 stitches, ML, k2.
Row 10: Purl.
Row 11: K1, (ML, k1) to end.
Row 12: P1, m1, p3 (m1, p3) to end.
81 stitches
Row 13: K1, (ML, k1) to end.
Row 14: Purl.
Row 15: K2, (ML, k1) to last 3 stitches, ML, k2.
Row 16: Purl.
Row 17: (K1, m1) to last stitch, k1.
161 stitches
Cast off.

CARDIGAN
Back
Using 4mm (size 6) needles and B doubled, cast on 25 stitches.
Change to yarn A.
Row 1: K1, (p1, k1) to end.
Row 2: Repeat row 1.

Row 3: Knit.
Row 4: Purl.
Repeat rows 3 and 4 10 more times, ending with a wrong-side row.
Row 25: K4, cast off centre 17 stitches, knit to end.
Do not cast off. Leave the two sets of shoulder stitches on a holder.

Right front
Using 4mm (size 6) needles and B doubled, cast on 25 stitches.
Change to yarn A.
Row 1: K1, (p1, k1) to end.
Row 2: Repeat row 1.
Row 3: Knit.
Row 4: Purl to last stitch, k1.
Row 5: K1, k2togtbl, knit to end. *24 stitches*
Row 6: Purl to last 3 stitches, p2togtbl, k1.
23 stitches
Repeat rows 5 and 6 until 4 stitches remain.
Do not cast off. Leave the shoulder stitches on a holder.

Left front
Using 4mm (size 6) needles and B doubled, cast on 25 stitches.
Change to yarn A.
Row 1: K1, (p1, k1) to end.
Row 2: Repeat row 1.
Row 3: Knit.
Row 4: K1, purl to end.
Row 5: Knit to last 3 stitches, k2tog, k1.
Row 6: K1, p2tog, purl to end.
Repeat rows 5 and 6 until 4 stitches remain.

Do not cast off. Leave the shoulder stitches on a holder.

SLEEVES
Using 4mm (size 6) needles and B doubled, cast on 19 stitches.
Change to yarn A.
Row 1: K1, (p1, k1) to end.
Row 2: Repeat row 1.
Row 3: Knit.
Row 4: Purl.
Repeat rows 3 and 4 6 more times, ending with a wrong-side row.
Cast off.

BALLET SLIPPERS
Using 4mm (size 6) needles and A, cast on 4 stitches.
Row 1: Purl.
Row 2: K1, (m1, k1) to end. *7 stitches*
Repeat rows 1 and 2 once more. *13 stitches*
Row 5: Purl.
Row 6: K1, (m1, k2) to end. *19 stitches*
Row 7: Purl.
Row 8: (K4, m1) twice, k3, (m1, k4), m1, knit to end. *23 stitches*
Row 9: Purl.
Row 10: Knit.
Row 11: Purl.
Row 12: K8, turn and work on these 8 stitches only as follows:
Row 13: Purl.
Row 14: Knit.
Repeat rows 13 and 14 three more times.
Row 21: Purl.

Cast off.

Rejoin yarn to remaining stitches, cast off centre 7 stitches, and knit to end. Working on these 8 stitches only, continue as follows:

Next row: Purl.

Next row: Knit.

Repeat these 2 rows 3 more times.

Next row: Purl.

Cast off.

FINISHING

SKIRT

The skirt has been knitted all in one piece. Sew together the side seam.

CARDIGAN

Join both shoulder seams using the three-needle cast-off technique as described on page 26.

Sleeves

Fold sleeve in half lengthwise and mark the centre of the cast-off edge with a marker. Line up this marker with the shoulder seam and baste the sleeve in place. Now sew the sleeve to the body. Attach both sleeves in the same way. Join both side and sleeve seams.

BALLET SLIPPERS

Fold slipper in half and sew the two side edges together – this creates a seam at the centre back. Using a large sewing needle and the photograph as a guide, lace 35cm (13¾in) of ribbon up the front of each slipper.

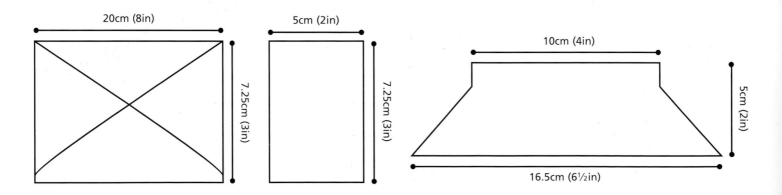

20cm (8in)

7.25cm (3in)

5cm (2in)

7.25cm (3in)

10cm (4in)

5cm (2in)

16.5cm (6½in)

Springtime Bear

Springtime Bear loves collecting wild flowers in her favourite yellow dress.

SKILL LEVEL
Simple

MATERIALS

For the dress
- 160m (175yd) 4ply yarn (A). The bear's outfit on page 32 uses one ball Rowan Calmer, 75% cotton, 25% acrylic, 50g (1oz), 160m (175yd), 494 Freesia

For the basket
- 115m (126yd) 4ply yarn (B). The bear's outfit on page 32 uses one ball Rowan Cotton Glace, 100% cotton, 50g (1oz), 115m (137yd), 730 Oyster

For the flowers
- 150m (126yd) 4ply yarn in four shades – two appropriate for flowers and two shades of green for leaves. The bear's outfit on page 32 uses small amounts Rowan Cotton Glace in the following shades: 724 Bubbles, 832 Persimmon, 814 Shoot, and 812 Ivy
- 210m (229yd) 4ply yarn in two shades appropriate for flowers. The bear's outfit on page 32 uses small amounts Rowan Kidsilk Haze, 70% super kid mohair, 30% silk, 25g (⅞oz), 210m (229yd) in the following shades: 606 Candy Girl and 579 Splendour
- 85m (93yd) aran weight yarn in a shade appropriate for flowers. The bear's outfit on page 32 uses small amount Rowan Handknit Cotton, 100% cotton, 50g (1oz), 85m (92yd), 305 Lupin
- 3.25mm and 4mm (sizes 3 and 6) needles (or size needed to obtain tension)
- Small amount of toy stuffing
- Large sewing needle

TENSION
25 stitches and 34 rows to 10cm (4in) using 4ply yarn and 4mm (size 6) needles, measured over stocking stitch.

DRESS (MAKE 2 FOR FRONT AND BACK)
Using 4mm (size 6) needles and A, cast on 43 stitches.
Row 1: K1, (p1, k1) to end.
Repeat row 1 three more times, ending with a wrong-side row.
Row 5: Knit.
Row 6: Purl.
Row 7: K1, k2togtbl, knit to last 3 stitches, k2tog, k1. *41 stitches*
Row 8: Purl.
Row 9: Knit.
Row 10: Purl.
Row 11: K1, k2togtbl, knit to last 3 stitches, k2tog, k1. *39 stitches*
Repeat rows 8 to 11 until 25 stitches remain.
Row 40: Purl.
Row 41: K9, turn and work on these 9 stitches only as follows:
Row 42: Purl.
Row 43: Knit to last 3 stitches, k2tog, k1.
8 stitches
Repeat rows 42 and 43 until 5 stitches remain.
Row 50: Purl.
Row 51: Knit.
Row 52: Purl.
Do not cast off. Leave the shoulder stitches on a holder.
With right side facing, rejoin yarn to remaining stitches and work as follows:
Next row: Cast off centre 7 stitches, knit to end.

Next row: Purl.
Next row: K1, k2togtbl, knit to end.
Repeat the last two rows until 5 stitches remain.
Next row: Purl.
Next row: Knit.
Next row: Purl.
Do not cast off. Leave the shoulder stitches on a holder.

NECKBAND
Join the right shoulder using the three-needle cast-off technique as described on page 26. With right side facing and 4mm (size 6) needles, pick up and knit 12 stitches down the left front of the neck, 8 stitches across the centre front, 12 stitches up the right front of the neck, 12 stitches down the right back of the neck, 8 stitches across the centre back, and 12 stitches up the left back of the neck. *64 stitches*
Row 1: (K1, p1) to end.
Cast off in seed stitch.

SLEEVES (MAKE 2)

Using 4mm (size 6) needles and A, cast on 19 stitches.

Row 1: K1, (p1, k1) to end.

Repeat this row once more, ending with a wrong-side row.

Row 3: Knit.

Row 4: Purl.

Repeat rows 3 and 4 four more times, ending with a wrong-side row.

Cast off.

BASKET

Side (make 2)

Using 3.25mm (size 3) needles and B, cast on 7 stitches.

Row 1: Purl.

Row 2: Increase in first stitch by knitting in the front and back of the stitch, yfwd, sl1, ybk, (k1, yfwd, sl1, ybk) to last stitch, increase in last stitch. *9 stitches*

Repeat rows 1 and 2 until there are 19 stitches.

Row 13: K1, (yfwd, sl1, ybk, k1) to end.

Row 14: Purl.

Row 15: K2, yfwd, sl1, ybk, (k1, yfwd, sl1, ybk) to last 2 stitches, k2.

Row 16: Purl.

Row 17: Purl. (This creates the ridge for a turn-over hem at the top of the basket.)

Row 18: Purl.

Row 19: Knit.

Row 20: Purl.

Cast off.

Lid

Using 3.25mm (size 3) needles and B, cast on 3 stitches.

Row 1: Purl.

Row 2: K1, (m1, k1) to end. *5 stitches*

Row 3: Purl.

Row 4: K1, m1, k3, m1, k1. *7 stitches*

Row 5: Purl.

Row 6: K1, m1, k5, m1, k1. *9 stitches*

Row 7: Purl.

Row 8: K1, m1, k7, m1, k1. *11 stitches*

Row 9: Purl.

Row 10: Knit.

Row 11: Purl.

Row 12: K1, k2togtbl, knit to last 3 stitches, k2tog, k1. *9 stitches*

Repeat rows 11 and 12 twice more. *5 stitches*

Row 17: Purl.

Row 18: K1, sl2, k1, p2sso, k1.

Row 19: Purl.

Cast off.

Handle

Using 3.25mm (size 3) needles and B, cast on 3 stitches.

Row 1: Knit.

Row 2: K1, p1, k1.

Repeat rows 1 and 2 until handle measures 14cm (5½in) from cast-on edge, ending with a wrong-side row.

Cast off.

FLOWERS

Flower with hot pink trim

Using 3.25mm (size 3) needles and Kidsilk Haze shade 606, cast on 49 stitches.

Change to Cotton Glace shade 724.

Row 1: K1, *k2, lift the first of these 2 stitches over the second, repeat from * to end. *25 stitches*

Row 2: (P2tog) to last stitch, p1. *13 stitches*

Do not cast off. Thread the yarn through the remaining stitches and pull, gathering it around into a flower shape, and then secure.

Pink flower

Using 3.25mm (size 3) needles and Cotton Glace shade 724, cast on 33 stitches.

Row 1: K1, *k2, lift the first of these 2 stitches over the second, repeat from * to end. *17 stitches*

Row 2: (P2tog) to last stitch, p1. *9 stitches*

Do not cast off. Thread the yarn through the remaining stitches and pull, gathering it around into a flower shape, and then secure.

Flower with dark purple trim (make 2)

Using 3.25mm (size 3) needles and Kidsilk Haze shade 579, cast on 29 stitches.
Change to Handknit Cotton shade 305.
Row 1: K1, *k2, lift the first of these 2 stitches over the second, repeat from * to end. *15 stitches*
Row 2: (P2tog) to last stitch, p1. *8 stitches*
Do not cast off. Thread the yarn through the remaining stitches and pull, gathering it around into a flower shape, and then secure.

Lilac flower

Using 3.25mm (size 3) needles and Handknit Cotton shade 305, cast on 25 stitches.
Row 1: K1, *k2, lift the first of these 2 stitches over the second, repeat from * to end. *13 stitches*
Row 2: (P2tog) to last stitch, p1. *7 stitches*
Do not cast off. Thread the yarn through the remaining stitches and pull, gathering it around into a flower shape, and then secure.

Orange flower

Using 3.25mm (size 3) needles and Cotton Glace shade 832, cast on 29 stitches.
Row 1: K1, *k2, lift the first of these 2 stitches over the second, repeat from * to end. *15 stitches*
Row 2: (P2tog) to last stitch, p1. *8 stitches*
Do not cast off. Thread the yarn through the remaining stitches and pull, gathering it around into a flower shape, and then secure.

LEAVES

Make five leaves – two in Cotton Glace shade 814, and three in Cotton Glace shade 812, as follows:
Using 3.25mm (size 3) needles, cast on 3 stitches.
Row 1: K1, p1, k1.
Row 2: K1, m1, k1, m1, k1. *5 stitches*
Row 3: K1, p3, k1.

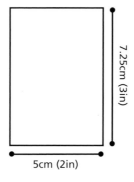

Row 4: K2, m1, k1, m1, k2. *7 stitches*
Row 5: K1, p5, k1.
Row 6: K2, sl2, k1, psso 2, k2. *5 stitches*
Row 7: K1, p3, k1.
Row 8: K1, sl2, k1, p2sso, k1. *3 stitches*
Row 9: Sl2, k1, p2sso. *1 stitch*
Fasten off.

FINISHING
DRESS
Join the left shoulder seam using the three-needle cast-off technique as described on page 26.

Sleeves
Fold sleeve in half lengthwise and mark the centre of the cast-off edge with a marker. Line up this marker with the shoulder seam and baste the sleeve in place. Then sew the sleeve to the body. Attach both sleeves in the same way.
Join both side and sleeve seams. Using

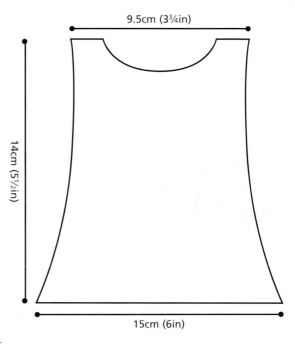

the photograph as a guide, sew one of the flowers with dark purple trim to the front left neck of the dress.

FLOWER BASKET
Basket
Fold hem inside the top of the basket and slip stitch into place. Do this for both sides. Join the two sides by sewing down one side, across the bottom and up the other side. Next, fill the basket with toy stuffing up to the slip-stitched hem. Insert the lid into the top of the basket (covering and sealing in the toy stuffing) and slip stitch to the hem. Now, using the photograph as a guide, sew the remaining flowers and leaves to the lid of the basket, making a nice arrangement.

Intermediate Medium-Sized Bear

Once you've mastered the simple bears, why not move on to this new friend? Doing the hula in Hawaii, cheering for your favourite sports team or shooting arrows as Robin Hood, this bear is ready for adventure.

FINISHED SIZE

Height: 27cm (10¾in)
Diameter (around body): 20cm (7¾in)

MATERIALS

Option A (Beige)

- 226m (246yd) DK weight yarn. The bear on page 38 uses two balls Rowan Wool Cotton, 50% wool, 50% cotton, 50g (1oz), 113m (123yd), 929 Dream

Option B (Cream)

- 226m (246yd) DK weight yarn. The bear on page 40 uses two balls Rowan Wool Cotton, 900 Antique
- 160m (175yd) 4ply yarn for facial features. The bear on page 38 uses a small amount Rowan Calmer, 75% cotton, 25% acrylic, 50g (1oz), 160m (175yd), 481 Coffee Bean
- 3.25mm (size 3) needles (or size needed to obtain tension)
- Large sewing needle
- Long sewing needle
- 50g (1¾oz) toy stuffing

TENSION

26 stitches and 32 rows to 10cm (4in) using 3.25mm (size 3) needles and DK weight yarn, measured over stocking stitch.

BODY

Sides (make 2)

Cast on 9 stitches.
Row 1 (RS): Knit.
Row 2: Purl.
Row 3: K4, m1, k1, m1, k4. *11 stitches*
Row 4: Purl.

Keeping shaping as set (increasing on either side of the centre stitch), repeat rows 3 and 4 until there are 21 stitches, ending with a wrong-side row.
Row 14: Knit.
Row 15: Purl.
Row 16: K10, m1, k1, m1, k10. *23 stitches*
Row 17: Purl.
Row 18: Knit.
Row 19: Purl.

Repeat rows 18 and 19 11 more times.
Row 42: K9, k2togtbl, k1, k2tog, knit to end. *21 stitches*
Row 43: Purl.
Row 44: K8, k2togtbl, k1, k2tog, knit to end. *19 stitches*
Row 45: P7, p2tog, p1, p2togtbl, purl to end. *17 stitches*
Row 46: K6, k2togtbl, k1, k2tog, knit to end. *15 stitches*
Row 47: P5, p2tog, p1, p2togtbl, purl to end. *13 stitches*
Row 48: K4, k2togtbl, k1, k2tog, knit to end. *11 stitches*
Row 49: P3, p2tog, p1, p2togtbl, purl to end. *9 stitches*
Row 50: (K2tog) 4 times, k1. *5 stitches*
Do not cast off. Thread yarn through the remaining stitches and pull together to secure.

HEAD

Left side

Using 3.25mm (size 3) needles, cast on 13 stitches.
Row 1: Knit.
Row 2: Purl.

Repeat rows 1 and 2 once more.
Row 5: K1, m1, knit to last stitch, m1, k1. *15 stitches*
Row 6: Purl.

Repeat rows 5 and 6 once more.
Row 9: Knit to last stitch, m1, k1. *18 stitches*
Row 10: P1, m1, purl to end. *19 stitches*

Repeat rows 9 and 10 once more.
Row 13: Knit to last stitch, m1, k1. *22 stitches*
Row 14: Purl.
Row 15: Knit.

Repeat rows 14 and 15 twice more.
Row 20: Cast off 5 stitches, purl to end. *17 stitches*
Row 21: Knit to last 3 stitches, k2tog, k1. *16 stitches*
Row 22: Cast off 4 stitches, purl to end. *12 stitches*
Row 23: Knit.
Row 24: Purl.
Row 25: K1, k2tog, knit to last 3 stitches, k2tog, k1. *10 stitches*
Row 26: P1, p2tog, purl to last 3 stitches, p2tog, p1. *8 stitches*
Cast off.

Right side

Using 3.25mm (size 3) needles, cast on 13 stitches.
Row 1: Knit.
Row 2: Purl.
Row 3: Knit.
Row 4: P1, m1, purl to last stitch, m1, p1. *15 stitches*
Row 5: Knit.

Repeat rows 4 and 5 once more.
Row 8: Purl to last stitch, m1, p1. *18 stitches*
Row 9: K1, m1, knit to end. *19 stitches*
Repeat rows 8 and 9 once more.
Row 12: Purl to last stitch, m1, p1.
22 stitches
Row 13: Knit.
Row 14: Purl.
Repeat rows 13 and 14 twice more.
Next row: Cast off 5 stitches, knit to end.
17 stitches
Next row: Purl to last 3 stitches, p2tog, p1.
16 stitches
Next row: Cast off 4 stitches, knit to end.
12 stitches
Next row: Purl.
Next row: Knit.
Next row: P1, p2tog, purl to last 3 stitches,
p2tog, p1. *10 stitches*
Next row: K1, k2tog, knit to last 3 stitches,
k2tog, k1. *8 stitches*
Cast off.

GUSSET
Using 3.25mm (size 3) needles, cast on
4 stitches.
Row 1: Knit.
Row 2: Purl.
Row 3: K1, m1, k1, m1, k1, m1, k1. *7 stitches*
Row 4: Purl.
Row 5: K1, m1, knit to last stitch, m1, k1.
9 stitches
Repeat rows 4 and 5 twice more. *13 stitches*
Row 10: Purl.
Row 11: Knit.
Row 12: Purl.
Row 13: K1, m1, knit to last stitch, m1, k1.
15 stitches
Row 14: Purl.
Row 15: Knit.
Row 16: Purl.

Row 17: Knit.
Row 18: Purl.
Row 19: K1, m1, knit to last stitch, m1, k1.
17 stitches
Row 20: Purl.
Row 21: Knit.
Row 22: Purl.
Row 23: Knit.
Row 24: Purl.
Row 25: K2tog, knit to last 2 stitches, k2tog.
15 stitches
Row 26: Purl.
Row 27: K2tog, knit to last 2 stitches, k2tog.
13 stitches
Repeat rows 26 and 27 until 9 stitches remain.
Row 32: Purl.
Row 33: Knit.
Repeat rows 32 and 33 four more times.
Row 42: Purl.
Row 43: K2tog, knit to last 2 stitches, k2tog.
7 stitches
Row 44: Purl.
Repeat rows 43 and 44 twice more. *3 stitches*
Next row: Sl2, k1, p2sso.
Fasten off.

LEGS (MAKE 2)
Using 3.25mm (size 3) needles, cast on
17 stitches.
Row 1: Knit.
Row 2: Purl.
Row 3: K1, m1, knit to last stitch, m1, k1.
19 stitches
Repeat rows 2 and 3 once more. *21 stitches*
Row 6: Purl.
Row 7: Knit.
Row 8: Purl.
Repeat rows 7 and 8 five more times.
Row 19: K8, k2togtbl, k1, k2tog, k8.
19 stitches
Row 20: Purl.

Row 21: Knit.
Row 22: Purl.
Row 23: K9, m1, k1, m1, k9. *21 stitches*
Row 24: P10, m1, p1, m1, p10. *23 stitches*
Repeat rows 23 and 24 until there are 31
stitches.
Row 29: Knit.
Row 30: Purl.
Row 31: Knit.
Cast off.

FEET PADS (MAKE 2)
Using 3.25mm (size 3) needles, cast on
3 stitches. Work as for knitting the feet pads
on page 64.

ARMS (MAKE 4 PIECES)
Using 3.25mm (size 3) needles, cast on
3 stitches. Work as for knitting the inner arms
until * on page 64.
Repeat rows 7 and 8 12 more times, and then
row 7 again.
Row 32: K1, k2tog, k3, k2tog, k1. *7 stitches*
Row 33: Purl.
Row 34: K1, k2tog, k1, k2tog, k1. *5 stitches*
Do not cast off. Thread yarn through the
remaining stitches and pull together to secure.

EARS (MAKE 2)
Using 3.25mm (size 3) needles, cast on
7 stitches.
Row 1: Knit.

Row 2: K1, p5, k1.
Repeat rows 1 and 2 once more.
Row 5: K2tog, knit to last 2 stitches, k2tog.
5 stitches
Cast off and, **at the same time**, k2tog at each
end of the cast-off row. Leave a long enough
thread to shape the ear and to attach it to the
head.

FINISHING
HEAD
Starting at the cast-on edges, sew together the
gusset and left side of head until you reach the
tip of the snout. Attach the right side of the
head in the same way.

Starting at the tip of the snout, continue
sewing the seam until you are two-thirds of the
way along the two cast-on edges of the sides.
Using the opening that you have left, stuff the
head until it is firm (using the photograph as a
guide to help you to achieve a good shape).
Finally, weave the yarn around the side of the
opening and pull, gathering the seams
together (like a drawstring). Fasten securely.

Facial features
Using the brown yarn (Rowan Calmer shade
481), sew the bear's facial features as follows:

Eyes
Measure approximately 4cm (1⅝in) up each
gusset seam from the tip of the snout. Using a
long sewing needle, create each eye as
described under finishing the eyes, from *, on
page 64.

Nose and Mouth
Work as for finishing the nose and mouth on
page 65, but making the long single vertical
stitch 0.75cm (⅜in) long.

BODY
Work as for finishing the body on page 65.

ARMS
Each arm is made up of two pieces. Join the
two pieces starting at the top of the arm,
working down one side and then up the other,
leaving an opening for stuffing. Stuff the arm,
then fasten securely.

LEGS
Work as for finishing the legs on page 65.

EARS
Mark the position of the ears as follows:
Measure approximately 6cm (2⅜in) from the
tip of the snout. Work as for finishing the ears,
from *, on page 65.

ASSEMBLING YOUR BEAR
Work as for assembling the bear on page 65.

Hula Bear

Hula Bear can't wait to dance you away to exotic locations. Put a flower in her hair and she's ready to go!

SKILL LEVEL
Simple

MATERIALS
For the skirt
- 108m (118yd) lightweight DK yarn (A). The bear's outfit on page 38 uses one skein Rowan Summer Tweed, 70% silk, 30% cotton, 50g (1oz), 108m (118yd), 507 Rush

For the top
- 115m (126yd) lightweight DK yarn (B). The bear's outfit on page 38 uses one ball Rowan Cotton Glace, 100% cotton, 50g (1oz), 115m (137yd), 809 Pier

For the flowers
- 115m (126yd) lightweight DK yarn in three shades – two appropriate for flowers (C and D) and one appropriate for leaves (E). The bear's outfit on page 38 uses small amounts Rowan Cotton Glace, 741 Poppy (C), 832 Persimmon (D), 812 Ivy (E)
- One 7mm press fastener
- 3.25mm and 4.5mm (sizes 3 and 7) needles (or size needed to obtain tension)

TENSION
SKIRT
16 stitches and 23 rows to 10cm (4in) using 4.5mm (size 7) needles and lightweight DK yarn, measured over stocking stitch.

TOP
23 stitches and 32 rows to 10cm (4in) using 3.25mm (size 3) needles and lightweight DK yarn, measured over stocking stitch.

SKIRT

Using 4.5mm (size 7) needles and A, cast on 17 stitches.

Row 1: *Cast off 13 stitches, k4.

Row 2: Turn and k4, turn and cast on 13 stitches.

Repeat rows 1 and 2 until 19 sections have been worked, finishing with casting off 13 stitches, k4.

Next 4 rows: Knit.

Cast off.

TOP

Using 3.25mm (size 3) needles and B, cast on 44 stitches.

Row 1: Knit.

Row 2: Purl.

Repeat rows 1 and 2 four more times. Cast off.

Flowers (make two in C and one in D)

Using 3.25mm (size 3) needles, cast on 23 stitches.

Row 1: K1, *k2, lift the first of these 2 stitches over the second, repeat from * to end. *12 stitches*

Row 2: P1, (p2tog) to end. *6 stitches*

Do not cast off. Thread the yarn through the remaining stitches, then pull together.

Leaves (make 2)

Using 3.25mm (size 3) needles and E, cast on 3 stitches.

Row 1: K1, p1, k1.

Row 2: K1, m1, k1, m1, k1. *5 stitches*

Row 3: K1, p3, k1.

Row 4: K2, m1, k1, m1, k2. *7 stitches*

Row 5: K1, p5, k1.

Row 6: K2, sl2, k1, p2sso, k2. *5 stitches*

Row 7: K1, p3, k1.

Row 8: K1, sl2, k1, p2sso, k1. *3 stitches*

Row 9: Sl2, k1, p2sso. *1 stitch*

Fasten off.

FINISHING

SKIRT

The skirt has been knitted all in one piece. Sew the press fastener onto the inside of the waistband at the cast-off end. Sew the other half of the press fastener to the corresponding position on the outside of the waistband at the cast-on end.

TOP

The top has been knitted all in one piece. Sew the two sides together, creating a seam at the centre back.

FLOWERS

Using the photograph as a guide, stitch a red flower, a yellow flower, and two leaves to the front left-hand side of the skirt waistband. Stitch a red flower behind the bear's ear.

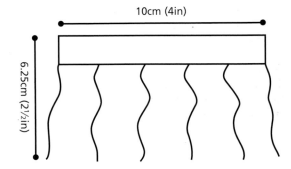

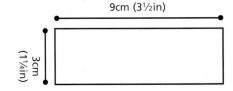

9cm (3½in)

3cm (1¼in)

10cm (4in)

6.25cm (2½in)

Robin Hood Bear

Ready to steal from the rich and give to the poor, Robin Hood Bear strides across Sherwood Forest with his quiver of arrows. With a jaunty hat and sturdy boots, he's sure to be everyone's hero.

SKILL LEVEL
Intermediate

MATERIALS
For the tunic
- 130m (142yd) DK weight yarn (A). The bear's outfit on this page uses one ball Rowan Classic Cashsoft DK, 57% extra fine merino, 33% microfibre, 10% cashmere, 50g (1oz), 130m (142yd), 523 Lichen

For the boots
- 130m (142yd) DK weight yarn (B). The bear's outfit on this page uses one ball Rowan Classic Cashsoft DK, 522 Cashew

For the tights and quiver
- 130m (142yd) DK weight yarn (C). The bear's outfit on this page uses one ball Rowan Classic Cashsoft DK, 517 Donkey
- 3.25mm and 4mm (sizes 3 and 6) needles (or size needed to obtain tension)
- 51cm (20in) brown leather thong
- Large sewing needle
- Toothpicks

TENSION
TIGHTS
23 stitches and 36 rows to 10cm (4in) using 3.25mm (size 3) needles and DK weight yarn, measured over stocking stitch.

TUNIC
22 stitches and 30 rows to 10cm (4in) using 4mm (size 6) needles and DK weight yarn, measured over stocking stitch.

BOOTS

22 stitches and 30 rows to 10cm (4in) using 4mm (size 6) needles and DK weight yarn, measured over stocking stitch.

TIGHTS

Front

Leg (make 2)

Using 3.25mm (size 3) needles and C, cast on 13 stitches.

Row 1: K1, (p1, k1) to end.
Row 2: P1, (k1, p1) to end.
Row 3: K1, (p1, k1) to end.
Row 4: Purl.
Row 5: Knit.
Row 6: Purl.

Repeat rows 5 and 6 9 more times, ending with a wrong-side row.

Do not cast off. Leave the stitches on a holder. Join the two legs of the front section as follows: With right sides facing, knit across 12 of the 13 stitches of left leg, knit the last stitch of the left leg together with the first stitch of the right leg, knit to end. *25 stitches*

Next row: Purl.
Next row: Knit.
Next row: Purl.
Repeat the last 2 rows seven more times.
Cast off.

Back

Work the same as for the Front.

TUNIC

Zigzag edging

Make 6 triangles as follows:

Using 4mm (size 6) needles and A, cast on 1 stitch.

Row 1: Increase in first stitch. *2 stitches*
Row 2: Increase purlwise into first stitch, purl to end. *3 stitches*
Row 3: Increase knitwise into first stitch, knit to end. *4 stitches*
Row 4: Increase purlwise into first stitch, purl to end. *5 stitches*
Row 5: Increase knitwise into first stitch, knit to end. *6 stitches*
Row 6: Increase purlwise into first stitch, purl to end. *7 stitches*
Row 7: Increase knitwise into first stitch, knit to end. *8 stitches*
Row 8: Increase purlwise into first stitch, purl to end. *9 stitches*
Row 9: Knit.

Do not cast off. Leave the stitches on a holder. Repeat until you have six triangles on holders.

Front

Join three of the triangles as follows: With wrong sides facing, purl across 9 stitches of one triangle, 9 stitches of second triangle, and then 9 stitches of third triangle. *27 stitches*
Row 2: Knit.
Row 3: Purl.
Row 4: Knit.
Row 5: Purl.
Row 6: K3, k3tog, (k6, k3tog) to last 3 stitches, k3. *21 stitches*
Row 7: Purl.
Row 8: Knit.
Row 9: Purl.

Repeat rows 8 and 9 eight more times, ending with a wrong-side row.

Shape front neck

Row 26: K10, turn and work as follows:
Row 27: K1, p9.
Row 28: K to last 3 stitches, k2tog, k1. *9 stitches*
Row 29: K1, purl to end.
Row 30: Knit.
Row 31: K1, purl to end.
Row 32: Knit to last 3 stitches, k2tog, k1. *8 stitches*
Repeat rows 29 through 32 twice more. *6 stitches*
Row 41: K1, p5.

Row 42: Knit.
Row 43: K1, p5.
Do not cast off. Leave the shoulder stitches on a holder.

Shape right neck
Row 26: Rejoing the yarn to the remaining stitches, cast off the centre stitch and knit to the end. *10 stitches*
Row 27: P9, k1.
Row 28: K1, k2togtbl, knit to end. *9 stitches*
Row 29: Purl to last stitch, k1.
Row 30: Knit.
Row 31: Purl to last stitch, k1.
Row 32: K1, k2togtbl, knit to end. *8 stitches*
Repeat rows 29 to 32 twice more. *6 stitches*
Row 41: P5, k1.
Row 42: Knit.
Row 43: P5, k1.
Do not cast off. Leave the shoulder stitches on a holder.

Back
Work rows 1 to 6 of the Front (page 40).
Row 7: Purl.
Row 8: Knit.
Row 9: Purl.
Repeat rows 8 and 9 16 more times, ending with a wrong-side row.
Next row: Knit.
Next row: P6, cast off centre 9 stitches, k6.
Do not cast off. Leave the two sets of shoulder stitches on a holder.

SLEEVES
Zigzag edging
Make eight triangles as follows:
Using 4mm (size 6) needles and A, cast on 1 stitch.
Row 1: Increase in first stitch. *2 stitches*
Row 2: Increase purlwise into first stitch, purl to end. *3 stitches*

Row 3: Increase knitwise into first stitch, knit to end. *4 stitches*
Row 4: Increase purlwise into first stitch, purl to end. *5 stitches*
Row 5: Increase knitwise into first stitch, knit to end. *6 stitches*
Row 6: Purl.
Do not cast off. Leave stitches on a holder. Repeat until you have eight triangles on holders.

Sleeves (make 2)
Join four of the triangles as follows: With right sides facing, knit across 6 stitches of one triangle, 6 stitches of a second triangle, 6 stitches of a third triangle, and 6 stitches of a fourth triangle. *24 stitches*
Row 2: Purl.
Row 3: K2, k2tog, (k4, k2tog) to last 2 stitches, k2. *20 stitches*
Row 4: Purl.
Row 5: Knit.
Row 6: Purl.
Repeat rows 5 and 6 three more times, ending with a wrong-side row.
Cast off.

BOOTS (MAKE 2)
Using 4mm (size 6) needles and B, cast on 21 stitches.
Row 1: Knit.
Row 2: Purl.
Repeat rows 1 and 2 once more.
Row 5: Purl. (This reverses the stocking stitch.)
Row 6: Knit.
Repeat rows 5 and 6 six more times.
Row 19: Purl.
Row 20: K8, k2togtbl, k1, k2tog, k8. *19 stitches*
Row 21: Purl.
Row 22: Knit.

Row 23: Purl.
Row 24: K9, m1, k1, m1, k9. *21 stitches*
Row 25: P10, m1, p1, m1, p10. *23 stitches*
Repeat rows 24 and 25 until there are 31 stitches.
Row 30: Knit.
Row 31: Purl.
Row 32: Knit.
Cast off.

Soles (make 2)
Using 4mm (size 6) needles and B, cast on 3 stitches.
Row 1: Purl.
Row 2: K1, m1, k1, m1, k1. *5 stitches*
Row 3: Purl.
Row 4: K1, m1, knit to last stitch, m1, k1. *7 stitches*
Repeat rows 3 and 4 once more. *9 stitches*
Row 7: Purl.
Row 8: Knit.
Row 9: Purl.
Repeat rows 8 and 9 twice more.
Row 14: K2, k2tog, k1, k2tog, k2. *7 stitches*
Row 15: Purl.
Row 16: K1, k2tog, k1, k2tog, k1. *5 stitches*
Cast off and, **at the same time**, k2tog at each end of the cast-off row.

QUIVER
Using 3.25mm (size 3) needles and C, cast on
4 stitches.
Row 1: Purl.
Row 2: K1, (m1, k1) to end. *7 stitches*
Row 3: Purl.
Row 4: K1, m1, k5, m1, k1. *9 stitches*
Row 5: Purl.
Row 6: K1, m1, k7, m1, k1. *11 stitches*
Row 7: Purl.
Row 8: K1, m1, k9, m1, k1. *13 stitches*
Row 9: Purl.
Row 10: K1, m1, k11, m1, k1. *15 stitches*
Row 11: Purl.
Row 12: Knit.
Row 13: Purl.
Repeat rows 12 and 13 four more times,
ending with a wrong-side row.
Cast off.

HAT
Left side
Using 3.25mm (size 3) needles and A, cast on
15 stitches.
Row 1: Knit.
Row 2: Purl.
Row 3: Knit to last 2 stitches, k2tog.
14 stitches
Row 4: Purl.
Repeat rows 3 and 4 until 12 stitches remain.
Next row: Knit to last 2 stitches, k2tog.
11 stitches
Next row: P2tog, purl to end. *10 stitches*
Repeat the last 2 rows until 6 stitches remain.
Cast off.

Right side
Using 3.25mm (size 3) needles and A, cast on
15 stitches.
Row 1: Knit.
Row 2: Purl.
Row 3: K2tog, knit to end. *14 stitches*
Row 4: Purl.
Repeat the last 2 rows until 12 stitches remain.
Next row: K2tog, knit to end. *11 stitches*
Next row: Purl to last 2 stitches, p2tog.
10 stitches
Repeat the last 2 rows until 6 stitches remain.
Cast off.

Back section
Using 3.25mm (size 3) needles and A, cast on
7 stitches.
Row 1: Knit.
Row 2: Purl.
Repeat rows 1 and 2 twice more, ending with
a wrong-side row.
Next row: K2tog, knit to last 2 stitches, k2tog.
5 stitches
Next row: Purl.
Next row: K2tog, k1, k2tog. *3 stitches*
Next row: Purl.

Next row: Sl2, k1, p2sso.
Fasten off.

FINISHING
TIGHTS
Join front and back of the tights as follows:
Sew the outer side seams – start at the top
(cast-off edge) and work down to the bottom
(cast-on edge). Now join the inner-leg seams.
Starting at the cast-on edge of the right leg,
work up to the top, and then work down the
corresponding seam of the left leg.

TUNIC
Join shoulder seams using the three-needle
cast-off as described on page 26.
Sleeves
Fold sleeve in half lengthwise and mark the
centre of the cast-off edge with a stitch marker.
Line up this marker with the shoulder seam and
baste the sleeve in place. Then sew the sleeve
to the body. Attach both sleeves in the same
way. Join both side and sleeve seams.

HAT
Join the left and right sides by sewing the
two shaped edges together. Then sew the left
edge of the back section to the straight edge
of the left side, and the right edge of the back
section to the straight edge of the right side.
The cast-on edge of the two side edges will
naturally curl, and this creates the brim.

BOOTS
Fold each boot in half lengthwise and, starting
at row 5 (where the stocking stitch has been
reversed), sew the two side edges together to
form a seam which runs down the back of the
boot. Attach the sole by sewing around the
edges of the sole, and joining it to the cast-off
edge of the boot. Fold down the top part of
the boot.

QUIVER

Fold the quiver in half lengthwise and sew the two side edges together, forming a seam that runs down the back of the quiver. Using the photograph as a guide, thread a length of leather thong through the top of the quiver as follows: Using a large sewing needle, thread the leather in through the quiver just to the right of the seam and then back out just to the left of the seam. Leave long lengths and tie in a knot. The quiver can then be carried over the bear's shoulder. Fill the quiver with toothpick arrows.

BELT

Using the photograph as a guide, tie a length of leather thong around the waist and tie in a knot.

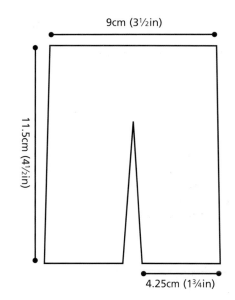

9cm (3½in)

11.5cm (4½in)

4.25cm (1¾in)

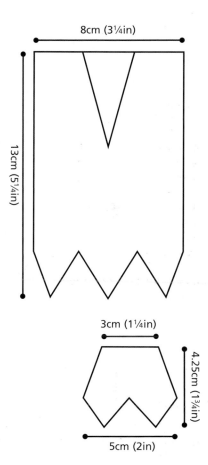

8cm (3¼in)

13cm (5¼in)

3cm (1¼in)

4.25cm (1¾in)

5cm (2in)

Cheerleader Bear

With her cute little pom-poms and uniform, Cheerleader Bear will lend her support to your school or favourite sports team. Why not dress her in your team colours?

SKILL LEVEL
Simple

MATERIALS
For the skirt and sweater
- 85m (93yd) aran weight yarn (A). The bear's outfit opposite uses one ball Rowan Handknit Cotton, 100% cotton, 50g (1oz), 85m (93yd), 263 Bleached

For the skirt, sweater and pom-poms
- 85m (93yd) aran weight yarn (B). The bear's outfit opposite uses one ball Rowan Handknit Cotton, 305 Lupin
- 3.25mm and 4mm (sizes 3 and 6) needles (or size needed to obtain tension)
- Large Sewing needle

TENSION
20 stitches and 28 rows to 10cm (4in) using 4mm (size 6) needles and aran weight yarn measured over stocking stitch.

SKIRT
Using 3.25mm (size 3) needles and A, cast on 46 stitches.
Change to yarn B.
Row 1: Knit.
Row 2: Purl.
Change to yarn A.
Row 3: Knit.
Row 4: Purl.
Row 6: Knit.
Row 7: Purl.
Row 8: K3, k2tog, (k4, k2tog) to last 3 stitches, k3. *37 stitches*
Row 9: Purl.

Row 10: K2, k2tog, k3, (k2tog, k3) to end. *30 stitches*
Row 11: Purl.
Row 12: K2, (k2tog, k2) to end. *23 stitches*
Row 13: Purl.
Row 14: K2, k2tog, knit to last 4 stitches, k2tog, k2. *21 stitches*
Row 15: Purl.
Row 16: Knit.
Row 17: Purl.
Row 18: Knit.
Cast off.

SWEATER
Back
Using 3.25mm (size 3) needles and A, cast on 23 stitches.
Row 1: (K1, p1) to last stitch, k1.
Row 2: (P1, k1) to last stitch, p1.
Change to yarn B.
Row 3: Knit.
Change to yarn A.
Row 4: Purl.
Row 5: Knit.
Row 6: Purl.
Repeat rows 5 and 6 10 more times.
Next row: K5, cast off centre 13 stitches, k5.
Do not cast off. Leave the shoulder stitches on a holder.
With right side facing, rejoin yarn to one set of the remaining 5 stitches and work as follows:
Next row: Purl.
Next row: Knit.
Do not cast off. Leave the shoulder stitches on a holder.
Repeat for the other shoulder.

SLEEVES (MAKE 2)

Using 3.25mm (size 3) needles and A, cast on 46 stitches.

Row 1: (K1, p1) to end.

Repeat last row once more.

Change to yarn B.

Row 3: Knit.

Change to yarn A.

Row 4: Purl.

Row 5: Knit.

Row 6: Purl.

Repeat rows 5 and 6 three more times.

Cast off.

FINISHING

SKIRT

The skirt has been knitted in two pieces. Sew together the two side seams.

SWEATER

Join the right shoulder seam using the three-needle cast-off technique as described on page 26.

With right sides facing and using B and 3.25mm (size 3) needles, pick up and knit 13 stitches down the right front of the neck, 13 stitches up the left front of the neck, and 14 stitches from the back of the neck. *40 stitches* Cast off.

Join left shoulder, using the three-needle cast-off technique as described on page 26.

Sleeves

Fold sleeve in half lengthwise and mark the centre of the cast-off edge with a stitch marker. Line up this marker with the shoulder seam and baste the sleeve in place. Now sew the sleeve to the body. Attach both sleeves in the same way.

Join both side and sleeve seams.

Front

Using 3.25mm (size 3) needles and A, cast on 23 stitches.

Row 1: (K1, p1) to last stitch, k1.

Row 2: (P1, k1) to last stitch, p1.

Change to yarn B.

Row 3: Knit.

Change to yarn A.

Row 4: Purl.

Row 5: Knit.

Row 6: Purl.

Repeat rows 5 and 6 four more times.

Row 11: K11, turn and work on these 11 stitches only as follows:

Row 12: Cast off 1 stitch, purl to end. *10 stitches*

Row 13: Knit to last 3 stitches, k2tog, k1. *9 stitches*

Row 14: Purl.

Row 15: Knit to last 3 stitches, k2tog, k1. *8 stitches*

Repeat last 2 rows three more. *5 stitches*

Row 19: Purl.

Do not cast off. Leave the shoulder stitches on a holder.

With right side facing, rejoin yarn to the remaining stitches and work as follows:

Row 20: Cast off next stitch, knit to end. *11 stitches*

Row 21: Purl to last 3 stitches, p2togtbl, p1. *10 stitches*

Row 22: K1, k2togtbl, knit to end. *9 stitches*

Row 23: Purl.

Row 24: K1, k2togtbl, knit to end. *8 stitches*

Repeat last 2 rows 3 more times. *5 stitches*

Row 28: Purl.

Do not cast off. Break yarn and leave the shoulder stitches on a holder.

POM-POMS

Using B, make two pom-poms as follows: Cut two circles of card approximately 2cm (¾in) in diameter with a 1cm (⅜in)-diameter hole in the middle. Wind the yarn around the outside of the two circles of card until the hole in the centre is almost filled in. Next, cut slowly and carefully around the edges of the two pieces of card until all the yarn has been cut. Gently ease the pieces of card apart, **but before taking them off completely**, tie a piece of yarn in a secure knot around the centre of the pom-pom to hold it together. Now remove the card. Attach a loop of yarn to each pom-pom, big enough to fit around the bear's arms.

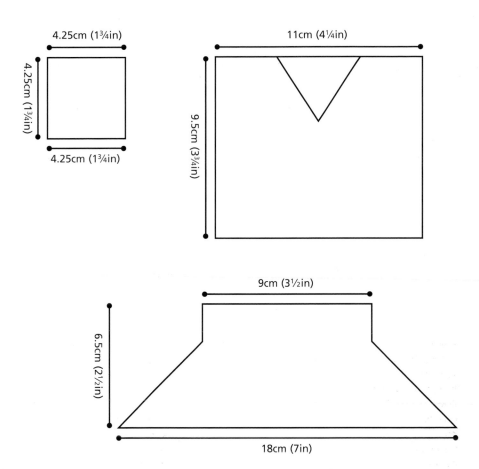

4.25cm (1¾in)

4.25cm (1¾in)

4.25cm (1¾in)

11cm (4¼in)

9.5cm (3¾in)

9cm (3½in)

6.5cm (2½in)

18cm (7in)

Intermediate Large Bear

This large bear is the perfect size for hugging! Kids and adults will just love this 35cm tall bear – and with so many outfits to choose from, you could spend hours playing dressing-up!

FINISHED SIZE
Height: 35cm (13¾in)
Diameter (around body): 30cm (12¾in)

MATERIALS
Option A (Beige)
- 130m (142yd) DK weight yarn. The bear on page 57 uses two balls Rowan Classic Cashsoft DK, 57% extra fine merino, 33% microfibre, 10% cashmere, 50g (1oz), 130m (142yd), 507 Savannah

Option B (Tweed)
- 130m (142yd) DK weight yarn. The bear on page 55 uses two balls Rowan Scottish Tweed DK, 100% wool, 50g (1oz), 130m (142yd), 025 Oatmeal
- 3.75mm (size 5) needles (or size needed to obtain tension)
- 160m (175yd) lightweight DK yarn for facial features. The bear on page 55 uses small amount Rowan Calmer, 75% cotton, 25% acrylic, 50g (1oz), 113m (124yd), 481 Coffee Bean
- Large sewing needle
- 85g (3oz) toy stuffing

TENSION
24 stitches and 32 rows to 10cm (4in) using 3.75mm (size 5) needles and DK weight yarn, measured over stocking stitch.

BODY
Sides (make 2)
Using 3.75mm (size 5) needles, cast on 11 stitches.
Row 1 (RS): Knit.

Row 2: Purl.
Row 3: K5, m1, k1, m1, k5. *13 stitches*
Row 4: Purl.
Keeping shaping as set (increasing on either side of the centre stitch), repeat rows 3 and 4 until there are 31 stitches.
Row 23: Knit.
Row 24: Purl.
Repeat rows 23 and 24 12 more times, ending with a wrong-side row.
Row 49: K11, (k2togtbl) twice, k1 (k2tog) twice, knit to end. *27 stitches*
Row 50: Purl.
Row 51: K9, (k2togtbl) twice, k1 (k2tog) twice, knit to end. *23 stitches*
Row 52: P9, p2tog, p1, p2togtbl, purl to end. *21 stitches*
Row 53: K8, k2togtbl, k1, k2tog, knit to end. *19 stitches*
Row 54: P7, p2tog, p1, p2togtbl, purl to end. *17 stitches*
Row 55: K6, k2togtbl, k1 k2tog, knit to end. *15 stitches*
Row 56: P5, p2tog, p1 p2togtbl, purl to end. *13 stitches*
Row 57: (P2tog) 3 times, p1, (p2tog) to end. *7 stitches*
Do not cast off. Thread yarn through the remaining stitches and pull together to secure.

HEAD
Right side
Using 3.75mm (size 5) needles, cast on 17 stitches.
Row 1: Knit.
Row 2: Purl.

Repeat rows 1 and 2 once more.
Row 5: K1, m1, knit to last stitch, m1, k1. *19 stitches*
Row 6: Purl.
Repeat rows 5 and 6 once more. *21 stitches*
Row 9: Knit.
Row 10: Purl to last stitch, m1, p1. *22 stitches*
Row 11: K1, m1, knit to end. *23 stitches*
Row 12: Purl to last stitch, m1, p1. *24 stitches*
Row 13: K1, m1, knit to end. *25 stitches*
Row 14: Purl to last stitch, m1, p1. *26 stitches*
Row 15: Knit.
Row 16: Purl.
Row 17: Knit.
Row 18: Purl.
Row 19: Knit.
Row 20: Purl.
Row 21: Knit.
Row 22: Purl.
Row 23: Cast off 6 stitches, knit to end. *20 stitches*
Row 24: Purl to last 3 stitches, p2tog, p1. *19 stitches*
Row 25: Knit.
Row 26: Purl.
Row 27: Cast off 5 stitches, knit to end. *14 stitches*
Row 28: Purl.
Row 29: Knit.
Row 30: Purl.
Row 31: Knit.
Row 32: Purl.
Row 33: K1, k2tog, knit to last 3 stitches, k2tog, k1. *12 stitches*

Row 34: P1, p2tog, purl to last 3 stitches, p2tog, p1. *10 stitches*
Cast off.

Left side
Using 3.75mm (size 5) needles, cast on 17 stitches.
Row 1: Knit.
Row 2: Purl.
Row 3: Knit.
Row 4: P1, m1, purl to last stitch, m1, p1. *19 stitches*
Row 5: Knit.
Repeat rows 4 and 5 once more. *21 stitches*
Row 8: Purl.
Row 9: Knit to last stitch, m1, k1. *22 stitches*
Row 10: P1, m1, purl to end. *23 stitches*
Row 11: Knit to last stitch, m1, k1. *24 stitches*
Row 12: P1, m1, purl to end. *25 stitches*
Row 13: Knit to last stitch, m1, k1. *26 stitches*
Row 14: Purl.
Row 15: Knit.
Row 16: Purl.
Row 17: Knit.
Row 18: Purl.
Row 19: Knit.
Row 20: Purl.
Row 21: Knit.
Row 22: Cast off 6 stitches, purl to end. *20 stitches*
Row 23: Knit to last 3 stitches, k2tog, k1. *19 stitches*
Row 24: Purl.
Row 25: Knit.
Row 26: Cast off 5 stitches, purl to end. *14 stitches*
Row 27: Knit.
Row 28: Purl.
Row 29: Knit.
Row 30: Purl.

Row 31: Knit.
Row 32: P1, p2tog, purl to last 3 stitches, p2tog, p1. *12 stitches*
Row 33: K1, k2tog, knit to last 3 stitches, k2tog, k1. *10 stitches*
Cast off.

Head gusset
Using 3.75mm (size 5) needles, cast on 5 stitches.
Row 1: Knit.
Row 2: Purl.
Row 3: K1, m1, k1, m1, k1, m1, k1, m1, k1. *9 stitches*
Row 4: Purl.
Row 5: K1, m1, knit to last stitch, m1, k1. *11 stitches*
Repeat rows 4 and 5 twice more. *15 stitches*
Row 10: Purl.
Row 11: Knit.
Row 12: Purl.
Row 13: K1, m1, knit to last stitch, m1, k1. *17 stitches*
Row 14: Purl.
Row 15: Knit.
Row 16: Purl.
Row 17: Knit.
Row 18: Purl.
Row 19: Knit.
Row 20: Purl.
Row 21: K1, m1, knit to last stitch, m1, k1. *19 stitches*
Row 22: Purl.
Row 23: Knit.
Row 24: Purl.
Row 25: Knit.
Row 26: Purl.
Row 27: Knit.
Row 28: Purl.
Row 29: Knit.
Row 30: Purl.

Row 31: K2tog, knit to last 2 stitches, k2tog. *17 stitches*
Row 32: Purl.
Row 33: K2tog, knit to last 2 stitches, k2tog. *15 stitches*
Repeat rows 32 and 33 until 9 stitches remain.
Next row: Purl.
Next row: Knit.
Repeat the last 2 rows 4 more times.
Next row: Purl.
Next row: K2tog, knit to last 2 stitches, k2tog. *7 stitches*
Next row: Purl.
Repeat the last 2 rows twice more.
Next row: Sl2, k1, p2sso.
Fasten off.

LEGS (MAKE 2)
Using 3.75mm (size 5) needles, cast on 19 stitches.
Row 1: Knit.
Row 2: Purl.
Row 3: K1, m1, knit to last stitch, m1, k1. *21 stitches*
Repeat rows 2 and 3 once more. *23 stitches*
Row 6: Purl
Row 7: Knit.
Row 8: Purl.
Repeat rows 7 and 8 eight more times.

Row 25: K9, k2togtbl, k1, k2tog, k9.
21 stitches
Row 26: P8, p2tog, p1, p2togtbl, p8.
19 stitches
Row 27: Knit.
Row 28: Purl.
Row 29: K9, m1, k1, m1, k9. *21 stitches*
Row 30: P10, m1, p1, m1, p10. *23 stitches*
Keeping shaping as set (increasing on either side of the centre stitch), repeat rows 29 and 30 until there are 31 stitches.
Next row: Knit.
Next row: Purl.
Next row: Knit.
Next row: Purl.
Next row: Knit.
Cast off.

FEET PADS (MAKE 2)
Using 3.75mm (size 5) needles, cast on 4 stitches.
Row 1: Purl.
Row 2: K1, (m1, k1) to end. *7 stitches*
Row 3: Purl.
Row 4: K1, m1, knit to last stitch, m1, k1. *9 stitches*
Repeat rows 3 and 4 once more. *11 stitches*
Next row: Purl.
Next row: Knit.
Next row: Purl.
Repeat the last 2 rows three more times.
Next row: K2, k2tog, k3, k2tog, k2. *9 stitches*
Next row: Purl.
Next row: K2, k2tog, k1, k2tog, k2. *7 stitches*
Cast off and, **at the same time**, k2tog at each end of cast-off row.

ARMS (MAKE 4)
Using 3.75mm (size 5) needles, cast on 4 stitches.
Row 1: Purl.
Row 2: K1 (m1, k1) to end. *7 stitches*
Row 3: Purl.
Row 4: K1, m1, k5, m1, k1. *9 stitches*
Row 5: Purl.
Row 6: K1, m1, k7, m1, k1. *11 stitches*
Row 7: Purl.
Row 8: Knit.
Repeat rows 7 and 8 14 more times, and then row 7 once more.
Next row: K1, k2tog, k5, k2tog, k1. *9 stitches*
Next row: Purl.
Next row: K1, k2tog, k3, k2tog, k1. *7 stitches*
Do not cast off. Thread yarn through the remaining stitches and pull together to secure.

EARS (MAKE 2)
Using 3.25mm (size 3) needles cast on 9 stitches.
Row 1: Knit.
Row 2: K1, p7, k1.
Rep rows 1 and 2 once more.
Row 5: K2tog, knit to last 2 stitches, k2tog. *7 stitches*
Row 6: P2tog, purl to last 2 stitches, p2tog. *5 stitches*
Cast off and, **at the same time**, k2tog at each end of cast-off row. Leave a long enough thread to shape ear and attach it to the head.

FINISHING
HEAD
Work as for finishing the head on page 36.

FACIAL FEATURES
Using the brown yarn (Rowan Calmer shade 481), sew the bear's facial features as follows:

Eyes
Work as for finishing the eyes on page 64.

Nose and Mouth
Work as for finishing the nose and mouth on page 65 but make the single vertical stitch 1.5cm (⅝in) long and the two diagonal stitches 0.75cm (¼in) long.

BODY
Work as for finishing the body on page 65, stuffing the bear to approximately 30cm (11¾in) in diameter.

ARMS
Work as for finishing the arms on page 36.

LEGS
Work as for finishing the legs on page 65.

EARS
Mark the position of the ears as follows: Measure approximately 8cm (3¼in) from the tip of the snout. Work as for finishing the ears from * on page 65.

Using the long tail that you left when casting off, give the ear some shape by sewing the tail around the outer edge of the ear, then using the same thread to attach to the head.

ASSEMBLING THE BEAR
Work as for assembling the bear on page 65, but sew the legs approximately 2cm (¾in) from the beginning of the side shaping.

Fisherman Bear

With his hat, cable-knit sweater and a cute little fish on the end of his line, Fisherman Bear is quite a catch. Any fishing fan would be delighted to get Fisherman Bear as a gift – if you can part with him!

SKILL LEVEL
Intermediate

MATERIALS
For the sweater
- 125m (137yd) DK weight yarn (A). The bear's outfit on this page uses one ball Rowan Pure Wool DK, 100% wool, 50g (1oz), 125m (136yd), shade 0121 Glade

For the trousers
- 130m(142yd) DK weight yarn (B). The bear's outfit on this page uses one ball Rowan Classic Cashsoft DK, 57% extra fine merino, 33% microfibre, 10% cashmere, 50g (1oz), 130m (142yd), 522 Cashew

For the wellies and hat
- 113m (123yd) DK weight yarn (C). The bear's outfit on this page uses one ball Rowan Wool Cotton, 50% wool, 50% cotton, 50g (1oz), 113m (123yd), 907 Deepest Olive

For the fish
- 115m (126yd) 4ply yarn for the fish (D). The bear's outfit on this page uses small amount Rowan Cotton Glace, 100% cotton, 50g (1oz), 115m (137yd), 832 Persimmon
- 3.25mm and 4mm (sizes 3 and 6) needles (or size needed to obtain tension)
- Two 10mm buttons, such as Rowan 00408
- Two 7mm press fasteners
- Thin wooden dowelling, approximately 25cm (10in) long
- Black sewing thread
- Sewing needle
- 10cm (4in) 28-gauge craft wire
- Cable needle

TENSION

SWEATER
22 stitches and 30 rows to 10cm (14in) using 4mm (size 6) needles and DK weight yarn, measured over stocking stitch.

TROUSERS
22 stitches and 30 rows to 10cm (4in) using 4mm (size 6) needles and DK weight yarn, measured over stocking stitch.

HAT AND WELLIES
22 stitches and 30 rows to 10cm (4in) using 4mm (size 6) needles and DK weight yarn, measured over stocking stitch.

ABBREVIATION
C6B Cable 6 back: Slip the next 3 stitches onto a cable needle and hold these at the back of the work, knit 3 from the left-hand needle, and then knit the 3 stitches from the cable needle.

TROUSERS

Front
Leg (make 2)
Using 3.25mm (size 3) needles and B, cast on 19 stitches.
Row 1: K1, (p1, k1) to end.
Row 2: P1, (k1, p1) to end.
Repeat rows 1 and 2 once more.
Row 5: K2, m1, (k5, m1) to last 2 stitches, k2. *23 stitches*

Row 6: Purl.
Row 7: Knit.
Row 8: Purl.
Repeat rows 7 and 8 eight more times, ending with a wrong-side row.
Do not cast off. Leave the stitches on a holder.

Join the two legs of the front as follows:
With right sides facing, knit across 22 stitches of the left leg, knit the last stitch of the left leg together with the first stitch of the right leg, knit to end. *45 stitches*
Row 2: Purl.
Row 3: K4, k2tog, (k3, k2tog) to last 4 stitches, k4. *37 stitches*
Row 4: Purl.
Row 5: Knit.
Repeat rows 4 and 5 nine more times, ending with right-side row.
Row 24 (WS): Knit (this creates a ridge for the turn-over hem at the top of the trousers).
Row 25: Knit.
Row 26: Purl.
Row 27: Knit.
Cast off.

Back
Work the same as for the Front of the trousers.

Straps (make 2)
Using 3.25mm (size 3) needles and B, cast on

5 stitches.
Row 1: Knit.
Row 2: K1, p3, k1.
Repeat rows 1 and 2 until the piece measures 31cm (12⅛in) from cast-on edge, ending with a wrong-side row.
Cast off.

SWEATER

Back
Using 3.25mm (size 3) needles and A, cast on 38 stitches.
Row 1: K2, (p2, k2) to end.
Row 2: P2, (k2, p2) to end.
Row 3: As row 1.
Row 4: Work in rib pattern for 1 stitch, m1, (work in rib pattern for 5 stitches, m1) seven times, work in rib pattern for 2 stitches. *46 stitches*
Repeat row 4 three more times, ending with a wrong-side row.
Change to 4mm (size 6) needles.
Row 8: *K1, (p1, k1) three times, k6, repeat from * twice more, k1, (p1, k1) to end.
Row 9: K1, (p1, k1) three times, *p6, k1, (p1, k1) three times, repeat from * to end.
Row 10: K1, (p1, k1) three times, *k6, k1, (p1, k1) three times, repeat from * to end.
Row 11: Work as for row 9.
Row 12: K1, (p1, k1) three times, *C6B, k1, (p1, k1) three times, repeat from * to end.

Row 13: Work as for row 9.
Row 14: Work as for row 10.
Row 15: Work as for row 9.
Row 16: Work as for row 10.
Row 17: Work as for row 9.
Row 18: Work as for row 10.**
Repeat rows 9 to 14 five more times, then repeat rows 9 to 12 once more.
Next row: Work as for row 9.
Next row: Work in pattern for 9 stitches, cast off centre 28 stitches, work in pattern for 9 stitches.
Do not cast off. Leave both sets of shoulder stitches on holders.

Front

Work as for back until **.
Repeat rows 9 to 14 four more times.
Row 40: Work as for row 9.
Row 41: Work in pattern for 17 stitches, turn, and keeping pattern correct, work on these 17 stitches only as follows:
Row 42: Work in pattern to end.
Row 43: Work in pattern to last 2 stitches, k2tog.
Row 44: P2tog, work in pattern to end.
Repeat rows 43 and 44 three more times, ending with a wrong-side row.
Do not cast off. Leave the shoulder stitches on a holder.
Rejoin yarn to remaining stitches, cast off centre 12 stitches and work in pattern to end. Work on these 17 stitches as follows:
Row 42: Work in pattern to end.
Row 43: K2tog, work in pattern to end.
Row 44: Work in pattern to last 2 stitches, p2tog.
Repeat rows 43 and 44 three more times, ending with a wrong-side row.
Do not cast off. Leave the shoulder stitches on a holder.

Neckband

Join the right shoulder using the three-needle cast-off technique as described on page 26. With right side facing, using 3.25mm (size 3) needles and A, pick up and knit 10 stitches down the left front of the neck, 12 stitches across the centre front, 10 stitches up the right front of the neck, and 30 stitches across the back. *62 stitches*
Row 1: K2, (p2, k2) to end.
Row 2: P2, (k2, p2) to end.
Row 3: K2, (p2, k2) to end.
Cast off in rib.

SLEEVES (MAKE 2)

Using 3.25mm (size 3) needles and A, cast on 26 stitches.
Row 1: K2, (p2, k2) to end.
Row 2: P2, (k2, p2) to end.
Repeat rows 1 and 2 once more, ending with a wrong-side row.
Change to 4mm (size 6) needles.
Row 5: (K1, p1) to end.
Row 6: (P1, k1) to end.
Repeat rows 5 and 6 12 more times, ending with a wrong-side row.
Cast off in seed stitch.

WELLIES
Boot (make 2)

Using 4mm (size 6) needles and C, cast on 25 stitches.
Row 1: Knit.
Repeat this row three more times.
Row 5: Knit.
Row 6: Purl.
Repeat rows 5 and 6 four more times, ending with a wrong-side row.
Row 15: K12, m1, k1, m1, k12. *27 stitches*
Row 16: P13, m1, p1, m1, p13. *29 stitches*
Row 17: K14, m1, k1, m1, k14. *31 stitches*
Row 18: P15, m1, p1, m1, p15. *33 stitches*

Row 19: K16, m1, k1, m1, k16. *35 stitches*
Row 20: Purl.
Row 21: Knit.
Row 22: Purl.
Row 23: Knit.
Row 24: Purl.
Cast off.

Sole (make 2)

Using 4mm (size 6) needles and C, cast on 4 stitches.
Row 1: Knit.
Row 2: K1, (m1, k1) to end. *7 stitches*
Row 3: Knit.
Row 4: K1, m1, knit to last stitch, m1, k1. *9 stitches*
Row 5: Knit.
Row 6: K1, m1, knit to last stitch, m1, k1. *11 stitches*
Row 7: Knit.
Repeat row 7 seven more times
Next row: K1, k2tog, knit to last 3 stitches, k2tog, k1. *9 stitches*
Next row: Knit.
Next row: K1, k2tog, knit to last 3 stitches, k2tog, k1. *7 stitches*
Next row: Knit.
Next row: K1, k2tog, k1, k2tog, k1. *5 stitches*

Cast off, decreasing 1 stitch at each end of cast-off row.

HAT

Using 4mm (size 6) needles and C, cast on 41 stitches.
Row 1 (WS): Purl.
Row 2: K2, k2tog, (k3, k2tog) to last 2 stitches, k2. *33 stitches*
Row 3: Purl.
Row 4: Knit.
Row 5: Purl.
Row 6: K1, (k2tog, k2) to end. *25 stitches*
Row 7: Purl.
Row 8: Knit.
Row 9: Purl.
Repeat rows 6 to 9 once more. *19 stitches*
Next row: K1, (k2tog, k1) to end. *13 stitches*
Next row: Purl.

Next row: K1, (k2tog, k1) to end. *9 stitches*
Do not cast off. Thread the yarn through the remaining stitches and pull together.

Brim

With right side facing, using 4mm (size 6) needles and C, pick up and knit 40 stitches along the cast-on edge of the hat.
Row 1: Knit.
Repeat row 1 twice more.
Row 4: K5, (m1, k5) to end. *47 stitches*
Row 5: Knit.
Repeat row 5 twice more.
Row 8: (K6, m1) to last 5 stitches, k5. *54 stitches*
Row 9: Knit.
Cast off.

FISH

Using 3.25mm (size 3) needles and D, cast on 3 stitches.
Row 1: K1, p1, k1.
Row 2: K1, m1, k1, m1, k1. *5 stitches*
Row 3: K1, p3, k1.
Row 4: K2, m1, k1, m1, k2. *7 stitches*
Row 5: K1, p5, k1.
Row 6: K3, m1, k1, m1, k3. *9 stitches*
Row 7: K1, p7, k1.
Row 8: K4, m1, k1, m1, k4. *11 stitches*
Row 9: K1, p9, k1.
Row 10: K4, sl2, k1, p2sso, k4. *9 stitches*
Row 11: K1, p7, k1
Row 12: K3, sl2, k1, p2sso, k5. *7 stitches*
Row 13: K1, p5, k1.
Row 14: K2, sl2, k1, p2sso, k2. *5 stitches*
Row 15: K1, p3, k1.
Row 16: K1, sl2, k1, p2sso, k1. *3 stitches*
Row 17: K1, p1, k1.
Row 18: K1, m1, k1, m1, k1. *5 stitches*
Row 19: K1, p3, k1.
Row 20: K1, (m1, k1) to end. *9 stitches*
Cast off.

FINISHING
TROUSERS

Both the front and back sections of the trousers have a hem at the top. Fold the hem inwards along the garter stitch ridge and slip stitch into place.

Join the front and back sections of the trousers as follows: Sew the outer seams. Start at the top (cast-off edge) and work down to the bottom (cast-on edge). Join the inner leg seams. Starting at the cast-on edge of the right leg, work up to the top, then work down the corresponding seam of the left leg.

Straps

At the cast-on edge of each strap, sew one half of each press fastener to the wrong side.
Sew each strap in place. Place four markers (to indicate where the straps are to be attached to the top of the trousers) as follows:
On the front of the trousers, measure 5cm (2in) in from the right side seam and place a marker. Measure 5cm (2in) in from the left side seam and place a marker. Repeat this on the back of the trousers.
Sew the remaining half of each press fastener to the outside of the front of the trousers as indicated by the two markers on this section.
Stitch the straps neatly and securely inside the top of the back section of the trousers as follows:
Sew the cast-off edge of one of the straps to the position of the right back marker, then sew the cast-off edge of the other strap to the position of the left back marker.
Now cross the straps so that the left back strap fastens to the right front press fastener and vice versa.
Sew the two buttons to the right side of each cast-on edge of the straps.

SWEATER

Join the left shoulder seam using the three-needle cast-off technique as described on page 26.

Sleeves

Fold sleeve in half lengthwise and mark the centre of the cast-off edge with a stitch marker. Line up this marker with the shoulder seam and baste the sleeve in place. Then sew the sleeve to the body. Attach both sleeves in the same way.
Join both side and sleeve seams.

HAT

Sew together the seam of the hat by working from the edge of the brim all the way to the top of the hat.

WELLIES

Fold each boot in half lengthwise and, starting at the cast-on edge, sew the two side edges together, forming a seam which runs down the back of the boot. Then attach the sole by sewing around the edges of the sole, joining it to the cast-off edge of the boot.

FISHING ROD

Using the photograph as a guide, make the fishing rod as follows: Cut a length of black sewing thread, approximately 25cm (10in). Starting about a quarter of the way along the wooden dowelling, stretch the thread so that it is parallel with the dowelling, ensuring that you have a good 7.5cm (3in) hanging free at the end, then secure by wrapping craft wire around the dowelling in three places, making sure the third is at the very tip of the rod. Sew the fish to the end of the thread.

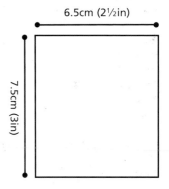

6.5cm (2½in)

7.5cm (3in)

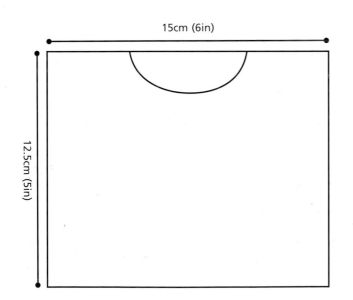

15cm (6in)

12.5cm (5in)

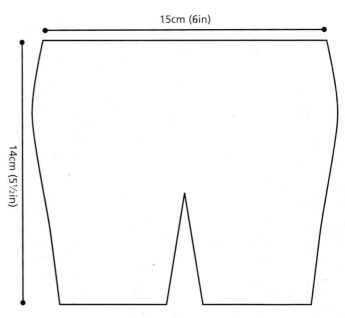

15cm (6in)

14cm (5½in)

Graduation Bear

Celebrate the end of high school or college with Graduation Bear. The cap and gown, which can be made in any school colour, make this bear the perfect gift for a graduating student.

SKILL LEVEL
Simple

MATERIALS
For the gown
- 104m (112yd) 4ply yarn (A). The bear's outfit opposite uses two balls Rowan Classic Bamboo Soft, 100% bamboo, 50g (1oz), 102m (112yd), 115 Black

For the cap
- 102m (126yd) 4ply yarn (B). The bear's outfit opposite uses one ball Rowan Cotton Glace, 100% cotton, 50g (1oz), 115m (137yd), 727 Black
- 3.25mm and 3.75mm (sizes 3 and 5) needles (or size needed to obtain tension)
- Cardboard, 9x9cm (3½x3½in)
- One 7mm press fastener
- Plain white paper measuring 4x9cm (5x3½in)
- 10cm (4in) of red ribbon, approximately 3mm (⅛in) wide
- Large sewing needle

TENSION
25 stitches and 30 rows to 10cm (4in) using 3.75mm (size 5) needles and 4ply yarn, measured over stocking stitch.

GOWN
Using 3.75mm (size 5) needles and A, cast on 45 stitches.
Row 1: Knit.
Row 2: K1, purl to last stitch, k1.
Repeat rows 1 and 2 five more times, ending with a wrong-side row.

Row 13: K4, m1, k1, m1, (k6, m1, k1, m1) to last 5 stitches, k5. *57 stitches*
Row 14: K1, purl to last stitch, k1.
Row 15: Knit.
Row 16: K1, purl to last stitch, k1.
Row 17: K5, m1, k1, m1, (k8, m1, k1, m1) to last 6 stitches, k6. *69 stitches*
Row 18: K1, purl to last stitch, k1.
Row 19: Knit.
Row 20: K1, purl to last stitch, k1.
Row 21: Knit.
Row 22: K1, purl to last stitch, k1.
Row 23: K6, m1, k1, m1, (k10, m1, k1, m1) to last 7 stitches, k7. *81 stitches*
Row 24: K1, purl to last stitch, k1.
Row 25: K14, turn and work on these 14 stitches only as follows:
Row 26: K1, purl to last stitch, k1.
Row 27: Knit.
Row 28: K1, purl to last stitch, k1.
Repeat rows 27 and 28 11 more times.
Do not cast off. Leave these stitches on a holder.
With right side facing, rejoin yarn to the remaining stitches, knit 53, and turn. Work on these 53 stitches stitches only as follows:
Row 26: K1, purl to last stitch, k1.
Row 27: Knit.
Row 28: K1, purl to last stitch, k1.
Repeat last 2 rows 11 more times.
Do not cast off. Leave these stitches on a holder.
With right side facing, rejoin yarn to remaining 14 stitches. Work on these 14 stitches only as follows:
Next row: K1, purl to last stitch, k1.
Next row: Knit.

Next row: K1, purl to last stitch, k1.
Repeat last 2 rows 11 more times.
Do not cast off. Leave the stitches on a holder. You will now have three sets of stitches on holders. Join these three sections as follows: With right side facing, knit across 14 stitches from the left section, 53 stitches from the middle section, and 14 stitches from the right section. *81 stitches*
Next row: K1, purl to last stitch, k1.
Next row: Knit.
Next row: K1, purl to last stitch, k1.
Repeat the last 2 rows until the gown measures 27cm (10⅜in) from cast-on edge.
Cast off.

CAP
Mortar board (make 2)
Using 3.25mm (size 3) needles and B, cast on 23 stitches.
Row 1: Knit.
Row 2: Purl.
Repeat rows 1 and 2 14 more times, ending with a wrong-side row.
Cast off.

Band
Using 3.25mm (size 3) needles and B, cast on 9 stitches.
Row 1: Knit.
Row 2: Purl.
Repeat rows 1 and 2 until work measures 18cm (7in) from cast-on edge, ending with a wrong-side row.
Cast off.

SCROLL
Using the photograph as a guide, roll the paper lengthwise into a scroll and tie the ribbon around the centre, securing it with a bow.

FINISHING
GOWN
Sew the press fastener to the front opening of the gown, approximately 4cm (1⅝in) down from the cast-on edge. When the press fastener is fastened, the cast-on edges of the gown will curl naturally, creating a collar.

CAP
Sew both mortar board pieces together, joining three side seams and leaving the fourth open. Slip the cardboard inside, then join the final seam.

Create a circle with the band by sewing the cast-on edge to the cast-off edge. Centre the band underneath the mortar board and slip stitch into place.

Tassel
Cut four 24cm (9½in) lengths of yarn. Fold each length in half and then, with another piece of yarn, tie all four together at the looped end. Use this yarn to attach the tassel neatly and securely to the centre top of the cap.

11.5cm (4½in)

27cm (10¾in)

33.5cm (13in)

Aladdin Bear

With his cute bolero and baggy trousers, Aladdin Bear is ready to take you on a magic carpet ride. Boys and girls alike will love this bear – find a lamp for him to rub and see if his wish will be granted!

SKILL LEVEL
SIMPLE

MATERIALS
For the trousers
- 85m (93yd) aran weight yarn (A). The bear's outfit on page 60 uses one ball Rowan Handknit Cotton, 100% cotton, 50g (1oz), 85m (93yd), 263 Bleached

For the bolero
- 85m (93yd) aran weight yarn (B). The bear's outfit on page 60 uses one ball Rowan Handknit Cotton, 314 Decadent
- 3.25mm and 4mm (sizes 3 and 6) needles (or size needed to obtain tension)
- 35cm (14in) of gold ribbon, approximately 2.5cm (1in) wide
- Small piece of Velcro
- Large sewing needle

TENSION
20 stitches and 28 rows to 10cm (4in) using 4mm (size 6) needles and aran weight yarn, measured over stocking stitch.

TROUSERS
Front
Leg (make 2)
Using 3.25mm (size 3) needles and A, cast on 17 stitches.
Row 1: K1, (p1, k1) to end.
Row 2: P1, (k1, p1) to end.
Repeat rows 1 and 2 once more.
Change to 4mm (size 6) needles.
Row 5: K1, m1, (k5, m1) 3 times, k1. *21 stitches*
Row 6: Purl.

Row 7: Knit.
Row 8: Purl.
Repeat rows 7 and 8 six more times.
Do not cast off. Leave these stitches on a holder.
Join the two legs of the front as follows: With right sides facing and using 3.25mm (size 3) needles, knit across 20 stitches of left leg, knit the last stitch of the left leg together with the first stitch of the right leg, knit to end. *41 stitches*
Next row: Purl.
Next row: K5, k2tog, (k3, k2tog) to last 4 stitches, k4. *34 stitches*
Next row: Purl.
Next row: Knit.
Next row: Purl.
Repeat the last 2 rows 7 more times, ending with a wrong-side row.
Next row: (K1, p1) to end.
Repeat last row three more times, ending with a wrong-side row.
Cast off in rib pattern.

Back
Work as for the Front.

BOLERO (KNITTED ALL IN ONE PIECE)
Using 4mm (size 6) needles and B, cast on 27 stitches.
Row 1: Knit.
Row 2: K1, p25, k1.
Repeat rows 1 and 2 seven more times, ending with a wrong-side row.
Row 17: K8, turn and work on these 8 stitches only as follows:
Row 18: K1, p6, k1.

Row 19: Knit.
Row 20: K1, p6, k1.
Repeat rows 19 and 20 seven more times, ending with a wrong-side row.
Row 35: Knit to last 3 stitches, k2tog, k1. *7 stitches*
Row 36: K1, p2tog, purl to last stitch, k1. *6 stitches*
Repeat rows 35 and 36 once more. *4 stitches*
Row 39: K1, k2tog, k1. *3 stitches*
Row 40: K1, p1, k1.
Cast off.

With right side facing, rejoin yarn to remaining stitches, cast off centre 11 stitches and knit to end. Continue as follows:
Row 18: K1, p6, k1.
Row 19: Knit.
Row 20: K1, p6, k1.
Repeat rows 19 and 20 seven more times, ending with a wrong-side row.
Row 35: K1, k2togtbl, knit to end. *7 stitches*
Row 36: K1, purl to last 3 stitches, p2togtbl, k1. *6 stitches*

Repeat rows 35 and 36 once more. *4 stitches*
Row 39: K1, k2togtbl, k1. *3 stitches*
Row 40: K1, p1, k1.
Cast off.

FINISHING
TROUSERS
Join the front and back of the trousers as follows:
Sew the outer side seams. Start at the top (cast-off edge) and work down to the bottom (cast-on edge). Then join the inner leg seams. Starting at the cast-on edge of the right leg, work up to the top, and then work down the corresponding seam of the left leg.

BOLERO
Fold over the two narrow strips so that they become the two fronts of the bolero. Stitch into place by joining the cast-off edge of the right front to the base of the right side seam, and then the cast-off edge of the left front to the base of the left side seam.

WAISTBAND
Fix the ribbon around the waistband of the trousers and use Velcro to fasten.

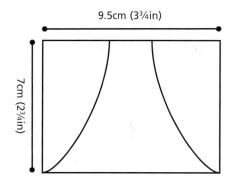

9.5cm (3¾in)

7cm (2¾in)

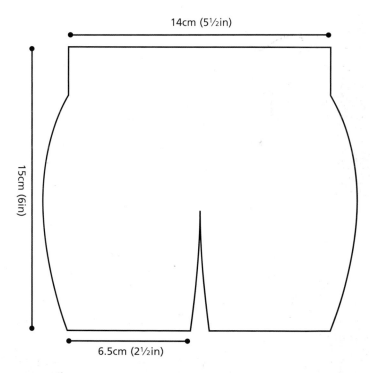

14cm (5½in)

15cm (6in)

6.5cm (2½in)

Complex Medium-Sized Bear

This complex bear is perfect for more advanced knitters. With more sophisticated shaping and a two-tone option, this bear is perfect as a collectable or for the kids to play with.

FINISHED SIZE
Height: 27cm (10⅝in)
Diameter (around body): 20.5cm (8in)

MATERIALS
Option A (Beige)
- 140m (153yd) aran weight yarn (A). The bear on page 70 uses one ball Rowan Kid Classic, 70% lambswool, 26% kid mohair, 4% nylon, 50g (1oz), 140m (153yd), 857 Oats
- 113m (123yd) DK weight yarn (B). The bear on page 70 uses one ball Rowan Wool Cotton, 50% wool, 50% cotton, 50g (1oz), 113m (123yd), 900 Antique

Option B (Cream)
- 140m (153yd) aran weight yarn (A). The bear on page 66 uses 1 ball Rowan Kid Classic, 828 Feather
- 113m (123yd) DK weight yarn (B). The bear on page 66 uses one ball Rowan Wool Cotton, 50% wool, 50% cotton, 50g (1oz), 113m (123yd), 929 Dream
- 160m (175yd) 4ply yarn for facial features. The bear on page 66 uses small amount Rowan Calmer, 75% cotton, 25% acrylic, 50g (1oz), 160m (175yd), 481 Coffee Bean
- 3.75mm (size 5) needles (or size needed to obtain tension)
- Large sewing needle
- 50g (1¾oz) toy stuffing

TENSION
25 stitches and 32 rows to 10cm (4in) using 3.75mm (size 5) needles and aran weight yarn, measured over stocking stitch.

BODY
Sides (make 2)
Using A, cast on 9 stitches.
Row 1 (RS): Purl.
Row 2: Knit.
Row 3: P4, m1, p1, m1, p4. *11 stitches*
Keeping shaping as set (increasing either side of centre stitch), repeat rows 2 and 3 until there are 21 stitches, ending with a right-side row.
Row 14: Knit.
Row 15: Purl.
Row 16: Knit.
Row 17: P10, m1, p1, m1, p10. *23 stitches*
Row 18: Knit.
Row 19: Purl. *
Repeat rows 18 and 19 11 more times, ending with a right-side row.
Row 42: Knit.
Row 43: P9, p2tog, p1, p2togtbl, purl to end. *21 stitches*
Row 44: Knit.
Row 45: P8, p2tog, p1, p2togtbl, purl to end. *19 stitches*
Row 46: K7, k2togtbl, k1, k2tog, knit to end. *17 stitches*
Row 47: P6, p2tog, p1, p2togtbl, purl to end. *15 stitches*
Row 48: K5, k2togtbl, k1, k2tog, knit to end. *13 stitches*
Row 49: P4, p2tog, p1, p2togtbl, purl to end. *11 stitches*
Row 50: K3, k2togtbl, k1, k2tog, knit to end. *9 stitches*
Row 51: (P2tog) 4 times, p1. *5 stitches*
Do not cast off. Thread yarn through the remaining stitches and pull together to secure.

HEAD
Left side
Using A, cast on 13 stitches.
Row 1: Purl.
Row 2: Knit.
Repeat rows 1 and 2 once more.
Row 5: P1, m1, purl to last stitch, m1, p1. *15 stitches*
Row 6: Knit.
Repeat last 2 rows once more. *17 stitches*
Row 9: Using A p15, using B k1, m1, k1. *18 stitches*
Row 10: Using B p1, m1, p2, using A knit to end. *19 stitches*
Row 11: Using A p15, using B k3, m1, k1. *20 stitches*
Row 12: Using B p1, m1, p2, using A knit to end. *21 stitches*
Row 13: Using A, p15, using B k5, m1, k1. *22 stitches*
Row 14: Using B p8, using A k14.
Row 15: Using A p13, using B k9.
Row 16: Using B p10, using A k12.
Row 17: Using A p12, using B k10.
Row 18: Using B p10, using A k12.
Row 19: Using A p12, using B k10.
Row 20: Using B, cast off 5 stitches, p5, using A k12. *17 stitches*
Row 21: Using A p12, using yarn B k2, k2tog, k1. *16 stitches*
Row 22: Keeping A and B as set, cast off 4 stitches, knit to end. *12 stitches*
Row 23: Purl.
Row 24: Knit.
Row 25: P1, p2tog, purl to last 3 stitches, p2tog, p1. *10 stitches*
Row 26: K1, k2tog, knit to last 3 stitches,

k2tog, k1. *8 stitches*
Cast off.

Right side
Using A, cast on 13 stitches.
Row 1: Purl.
Row 2: Knit.
Row 3: Purl.
Row 4: K1, m1, knit to last stitch, m1, k1.
15 stitches
Row 5: Purl.
Repeat rows 4 and 5 once more. *17 stitches*
Row 8: Using A k15, using B p1, m1, p1.
18 stitches
Row 9: Using B k1, m1, k2, using A purl to
end. *19 stitches*
Row 10: Using A k15, using B p3, m1, p1.
20 stitches
Row 11: Using B k1, m1, k4, using A purl to
end. *21 stitches*
Row 12: Using A k15, using B p5, m1, p1.
22 stitches
Row 13: Using B k8, using A p14.
Row 14: Using A k13, using B p9.
Row 15: Using B k10, using A p12.
Row 16: Using A k12, using B p10.
Row 17: Using B k10, using A p12.
Row 18: Using A k12, using B p10.
Row 19: Using B cast off 5 stitches, k5,
using A p12. *17 stitches*
Row 20: Using A k12, using B p2, p2tog, p1.
16 stitches
Row 21: Keeping yarns A and B as set, cast off
4 stitches, purl to end. *12 stitches*
Row 22: Knit.
Row 23: Purl.
Row 24: K1, k2tog, knit to last 3 stitches,
k2tog, k1. *10 stitches*
Row 25: P1, p2tog, purl to last 3 stitches,
p2tog, p1. *8 stitches*
Cast off.

Head gusset
Using A, cast on 4 stitches.
Row 1: Purl.
Row 2: Knit.
Row 3: P1 (m1, k1) to end. *7 stitches*
Row 4: Knit.
Row 5: P1, m1, purl to last stitch, m1, p1.
9 stitches
Repeat rows 4 and 5 twice more. *13 stitches*
Row 10: Knit.
Row 11: Purl.
Row 12: Knit.
Row 13: P1, m1, purl to last stitch, m1, p1.
15 stitches
Row 14: Knit.
Row 15: Purl.
Row 16: Knit.
Row 17: Purl.
Row 18: Knit.
Row 19: P1, m1, purl to last stitch, m1, p1.
17 stitches
Row 20: Knit.
Row 21: Purl.
Row 22: Knit.
Row 23: Purl.
Row 24: Knit.
Row 25: P2tog, purl to last 2 stitches, p2tog.
15 stitches
Row 26: Knit.
Row 27: P2tog, purl to last 2 stitches, p2tog.
13 stitches
Repeat rows 26 and 27 until 9 stitches remain.
Row 32: Knit.
Row 33: Purl.
Repeat rows 32 and 33 twice more.
Row 38: Knit.
Change to yarn B and continue as follows:
Row 39: Knit.
Row 40: Purl.
Row 41: Knit.
Repeat rows 40 and 41 once more.

Row 44: P2tog, purl to last 2 stitches, p2tog.
7 stitches
Row 45: Knit.
Repeat rows 44 and 45 twice more.
Row 50: Sl2, p1, p2sso.
Fasten off.

LEGS (MAKE 2)
Using A, cast on 17 stitches.
Row 1: Purl.
Row 2: Knit.
Row 3: P1, m1, purl to last stitch, m1, p1.
19 stitches
Repeat rows 2 and 3 once more. *21 stitches*
Row 6: Knit.
Row 7: Purl.
Row 8: Knit.
Repeat rows 7 and 8 six more times.
Row 21: P8, p2tog, p1, p2togtbl, p8.
19 stitches
Row 22: Knit.
Row 23: Purl.
Row 24: Knit.
Row 25: P9, m1, p1, m1, p9. *21 stitches*
Row 26: K10, m1, k1, m1, k10. *23 stitches*
Keeping shaping as set (increasing either side
of centre stitch), repeat rows 25 and 26 until
there are 31 stitches, ending with a wrong-side
row.
Next row: Purl.
Next row: Knit.
Next row: Purl.
Cast off.

FEET PADS (MAKE 2)

Using B, cast on 3 stitches.

Row 1: Purl.
Row 2: K1, m1, k1, m1, k1. *5 stitches*
Row 3: Purl.
Row 4: K1, m1, knit to last stitch, m1, k1. *7 stitches*
Repeat rows 3 and 4 once more. *9 stitches*
Row 7: Purl.
Row 8: Knit.
Row 9: Purl.
Repeat rows 8 and 9 twice more.
Row 14: K2, k2tog, k1, k2tog, k2. *7 stitches*
Row 15: Purl.
Row 16: K1, k2tog, k1, k2tog, k1. *5 stitches*
Cast off and, **at the same time**, k2tog at each end of the cast-off row.

ARMS

Inner arms (make 2)

Using B, cast on 3 stitches.

Row 1: Purl.
Row 2: K1, m1, k1, m1, k1. *5 stitches*
Row 3: Purl.
Row 4: K1, m1, k3, m1, k1. *7 stitches*
Row 5: Purl.
Row 6: K1, m1, k5, m1, k1. *9 stitches*
Row 7: Purl.
Row 8: Knit.
Row 9: Purl.
Change yarn to A and continue as follows:
Row 10: Knit.
Row 11: Knit.
Row 12: Purl.
Repeat last 2 rows 11 more times.
Next row: Knit.
Next row: P1, p2tog, p3, p2togtbl, p1. *7 stitches*
Next row: Knit.
Next row: P1, p2tog, p1, p2togtbl, p1. *5 stitches*

Do not cast off. Thread yarn through the remaining stitches and pull together to secure.

Outer arms (make 2)

Using A, cast on 3 stitches.

Row 1: Knit.
Row 2: P1, m1, p1, m1, p1. *5 stitches*
Row 3: Knit.
Row 4: P1, m1, p3, m1, p1. *7 stitches*
Row 5: Knit.
Row 6: P1, m1, p5, m1, p1. *9 stitches*
Row 7: Knit.
Row 8: Purl.
Repeat rows 7 and 8 13 more times.
Next row: Knit.
Next row: P1, p2tog, p3, p2togtbl, p1. *7 stitches*
Next row: Knit.
Next row: P1, p2tog, p1, p2togtbl, p1. *5 stitches*
Do not cast off. Thread yarn through the remaining stitches and pull together to secure.

EARS (MAKE 2)

Cast on 7 stitches.

Row 1: Knit.
Row 2: Purl.
Repeat rows 1 and 2 once more.
Row 5: K2tog, knit to last 2 stitches, k2tog *5 stitches*
Cast off and, **at the same time**, k2tog at each end of the cast-off row. Leave a long enough tail to shape the ear and attach it to the head.

FINISHING

HEAD

Using A and starting at the cast-on edges, sew together the gusset and left side of head until you reach the beginning of the snout. Change to yarn B and continue sewing the seam until you reach the tip of snout. Attach the right side of the head in the same way.
Using B and starting at the tip of the snout, sew the front seam of the two sides until you reach the end of the snout. Change to yarn A and continue sewing the seam until you are two-thirds of the way along the two cast-on edges of the sides. Using the opening that you have left, stuff the head until it is firm (using the photograph as a guide to help you to achieve a good shape). Finally, weave A around the side of the opening and pull, gathering the seams together (like a drawstring). Fasten securely.

FACIAL FEATURES

Using the brown yarn (Rowan Calmer shade 481), sew the bear's facial features as follows:

Eyes

Measure approximately 4.5cm (1¾in) up each gusset seam from the tip of the snout. *Use a long sewing needle to create each eye as follows: Leaving a long tail for securing, insert the needle just to the right of the gusset seam and then bring it out to just to the left of the gusset seam. Take the yarn back through once more in the same way. Then insert the needle into the original hole and, this time, take it down through the centre of the head and out through the underside. Now return to the long thread that you left at the beginning and thread this onto your needle. Insert it into the hole to the left of the gusset and take it down through the centre of the head and out through the underside. Pulling gently on these two yarns will set the eyes further into the bear's head, giving your bear's face character. When you have sewn both eyes, pull gently on these yarns to create a face you are happy with. Then secure the yarns firmly so as to keep the features you have created.

Nose and mouth

The nose is an upside-down triangle. Use the gusset seams where they taper to a point for the snout as a guide as to where you need to sew to get a good shape. Insert the needle into the left gusset seam and take it horizontally under the knitting and out through the right gusset seam. Now insert it into the left seam again but, this time, just below where you originally went in. Again, take it horizontally under the knitting and out of the right seam, just below the previous stitch. Continue in this way, shortening each consecutive stitch, until the nose tapers to a point at the tip of the snout. Next, starting at the tip of the snout, sew a long single stitch roughly 1.5cm (⅝in) down and insert the needle into the head, then bring it out 0.75cm (¼in) to the left and slightly lower. Create a diagonal single stitch by inserting the needle back in through the base of the 1.5cm (⅝in) vertical stitch. Then bring the needle back out approximately 0.75cm (¼in) to the right and slightly lower (opposite to last time) and create a second diagonal stitch by inserting the needle back in through the base of the 1.5cm (⅝in) vertical stitch. Take the needle down through the centre of the head and out through the underside. Fasten securely.

BODY

Sew the two pieces together as follows (the seams are at the centre front and centre back of the body): Starting at the cast-on edge, sew the first seam all the way to the top of the body. Sew the other seam in the same way, but stop approximately two-thirds of the way up. Join the cast-on edges of the two pieces. Using the opening that you have left, stuff the body until it is firm and roughly 20cm (7¾in) in diameter (using the photograph as a guide to help you to achieve a good shape). Sew up the remaining third of the second seam. Fasten securely.

ARMS

Each arm has an outer section and an inner section. The inner section has a paw pad in the contrasting yarn. Join the inner section to the outer section starting at the top of the arm, working down one side and then up the other, stopping approximately two-thirds of the way up. Then, using the opening you have left, stuff the arm until it is firm, then sew up the remaining third of the seam. Fasten securely.

LEGS

Each leg has been knitted in one piece and will have a foot pad attached at the sole. Fold the leg in half lengthwise and sew the two side edges together, forming a seam which runs down the back of the leg. When folding the leg in half, you will have folded the cast-on edge in half, too. Join these two edges together, creating a seam that runs across the top of the leg from front to back.
Using the opening that you have at the base of the foot, stuff the leg until it is firm (using the photograph as a guide to help you to achieve a good shape) and then attach the foot pad by sewing around the edges of the pad, joining it to the cast-off edge of the leg.

EARS

Mark the position of the ears as follows: Measure approximately 5cm (2in) from the beginning of the colour change of the snout, up the head seam. *Place the ear across the seam and attach as follows: Using the long tail that you left when casting off, give the ear some shape by sewing the tail around the outer edge of the ear and then use the same thread to attach to the head.

ASSEMBLING THE BEAR

Sew the head securely to the centre top of the body. Stitch the arms to the body at the beginning of the shoulder shaping. Sew the legs to the body approximately 1cm (⅜in) from the beginning of the side shaping.

Safari Bear

Join Safari Bear on the lookout for wild animals! With his butterfly net and khaki safari suit, he's definitely ready for adventure.

SKILL LEVEL
Simple

MATERIALS
For the shirt and shorts
- 85m (93yd) aran weight yarn (A). The bear's outfit opposite uses one ball Rowan Handknit Cotton, 100% cotton, 50g (1oz), 85m (93yd), 205 Line

For the butterfly
- 115m (126yd) aran weight yarn (B). The bear's outfit opposite uses one ball Rowan Cotton Glace, 100% cotton, 50g (1oz), 115m (137yd), 832 Persimmon
- 3mm, 3.25mm, and 4mm (sizes 2, 3, and 6) needles (or size needed to obtain tension)
- Six 5mm buttons, such as Rowan 00333
- Three 7mm press fasteners
- 15cm (6in) length of 28-gauge craft wire
- Craft glue
- Two 3mm black beads, such as Rowan 01017
- 12.5cm (5in) length of dowelling
- Small piece of netting fabric
- Small amount of white yarn
- Large sewing needle

TENSION
20 stitches and 28 rows to 10cm (4in) using 4mm (size 6) needles and aran weight yarn, measured over stocking stitch.

SHORTS
Front
Leg (make 2)
Using 4mm (size 6) needles and A, cast on 17 stitches.
Row 1: Knit.

Row 2: Purl.
Row 3: Purl (this creates a ridge for the hem and reverses the stocking stitch).
Row 4: Knit.
Row 5: Purl.
Repeat rows 4 and 5 five more times.
Do not cast off. Leave the stitches on a holder.
Join the two legs of the front as follows: With right sides facing, knit across 16 stitches of the left leg, knit the last stitch of the left leg together with the first stitch of the right leg, knit to end. *33 stitches*
Row 2: Purl.
Row 3: K2, k2tog, (k1, k2tog) to last 2 stiches, k2. *23 stitches*
Row 4: Purl.
Row 5: Knit.
Row 6: Purl.
Repeat rows 5 and 6 five more times, ending with a wrong-side row.
Row 17: K3, (k2tog, k3) to end. *19 stitches*
Row 18: Purl.
Cast off.

Back
Work as for the Front.

SHIRT
Back
Using 4mm (size 6) needles and A, cast on 25 stitches.
Row 1: Knit.
Row 2: Purl.
Repeat rows 1 and 2 14 more times, ending with a wrong-side row.
Next row: K7, cast off centre 11 stitches, k7.
Do not cast off. Leave the two sets of shoulder stitches on a holder.

Right front
Using 4mm (size 6) needles and A, cast on 14 stitches.
Row 1: Knit.
Row 2: P13, k1.
Repeat rows 1 and 2 10 more times, ending with a wrong-side row.
Row 23: Cast off 4 stitches, knit to end. *10 stitches*
Row 24: Purl.
Row 25: K1, k2togtbl, knit to end. *9 stitches*
Repeat rows 24 and 25 twice more. *7 stitches*
Row 30: Purl.
Row 31: Knit.
Do not cast off. Leave the shoulder stitches on a holder.

Left front
Using 4mm (size 6) needles and A, cast on 14 stitches.
Row 1: Knit.
Row 2: K1, p13.
Repeat rows 1 and 2 9 more times, ending with a wrong-side row.
Row 21: Knit.
Row 22: Cast off 4 stitches, purl to end. *10 stitches*
Row 23: Knit.
Row 24: K1, p2tog, purl to end. *9 stitches*
Repeat rows 23 and 24 twice more. *7 stitches*
Row 29: Knit.
Row 30: Purl.
Row 31: Knit.
Do not cast off. Leave the shoulder stitches on a holder.

Join both shoulder seams using the three-needle cast-off technique as described on page 26, then work the collar as follows: Using 3.25mm (size 3) needles and A, and with the wrong side facing, pick up and knit 13 stitches up the left of the neck, 15 stitches across the back, and 13 stitches down the right of the neck. *41 stitches*
Row 1: Purl.
Row 2: Knit.
Row 3: Purl.
Repeat rows 2 and 3 once more.
Cast off.

Sleeves
Using 4mm (size 6) needles and A, cast on 20 stitches.
Row 1: Knit.

Row 2: Purl.
Row 3: Purl (this creates a ridge for the hem and reverses the stocking stitch).
Row 4: Knit.
Row 5: Purl.
Repeat rows 4 and 5 five more times, ending with a wrong-side row.
Cast off.

Shirt Pockets
Using 3.25mm (size 3) needles and A, cast on 7 stitches.
Row 1: Knit.
Row 2: K1, p5, k1.
Repeat rows 1 and 2 three more times, ending with a wrong-side row.
Cast off.

Short Pockets
Using 3.25mm (size 3) needles and A, cast on 9 stitches.
Row 1: Knit.
Row 2: K1, p7, k1.
Repeat rows 1 and 2 four more times, ending with a wrong-side row.
Cast off.

BUTTERFLY
Using 3mm (size 2) needles and B, cast on 9 stitches.
Row 1: Knit.
Row 2: Purl.
Row 3: K2tog, k5, k2tog. *7 stitches*
Row 4: P2tog, p3, p2tog. *5 stitches*
Row 5: K2tog, k1, k2tog. *3 stitches*
Row 6: Purl.
Row 7: K1, m1, knit to last stitch, m1 , k1. *5 stitches*
Row 8: P1, m1, purl to last stitch, m1 , p1. *7 stitches*
Row 9: K1, m1, knit to last stitch, m1, k1. *9 stitches*
Row 10: Purl.
Row 11: Knit.
Cast off.

FINISHING
SHORTS
Both the front and back sections of the shorts have a hem at the bottom of each leg. Fold the hem outwards along the ridge and slip stitch into place on the right side of the shorts.
Join both front and back sections of the shorts as follows: Sew the outer seams. Start at the top (cast-off edge) and work down to the bottom (cast-on edge). Now join the inner leg seams. Starting at the cast-on edge of the right leg, work up to the top, and then work down the corresponding seam of the left leg.

Using the photograph as a guide, sew one button on each pocket. Sew pockets onto the shorts as in the photograph, positioning pockets over the side seams.

SHIRT
Sleeves
Both sleeves have a hem at the cast-on edge. Fold the hem outwards along the ridge and slip stitch into place on the right side of each sleeve.

Fold sleeve in half lengthwise and mark the centre of the cast-off edge with a stitch marker. Line up this marker with the shoulder seam and tack the sleeve in place. Now sew the sleeve to the body. Attach both sleeves in the same way.
Join both side and sleeve seams.

Using the photograph as a guide, sew buttons into place as follows: One on each pocket and one on each turn-back on the sleeves. Sew pockets onto the fronts, as in the photograph. Sew press fasteners to the front opening, positioning one just below the neck, one just above the cast-on edge, and the other in between.

BUTTERFLY
Cut a length of craft wire, twist it around the centre of the butterfly (the narrowest point), and bend the two ends so that they create the antennae. Attach a black bead to the top of each antenna.

BUTTERFLY NET
From the net fabric, cut a triangle measuring approximately 14cm (5½in) along its base, with the other two sides measuring approximately

7.5cm (2½in). Fold the triangle in half and join the two edges of the lower base edge. Carefully thread wire in and out of the other two edges and shape this edge into a circle, twisting the two ends of wire together where they meet. Using a small amount of white yarn, apply craft glue to hold the yarn in place, and using the photograph as a guide, wrap the length of yarn around one end of the dowelling, securing the net wire in place. Wrap another length of yarn around the other end of the dowelling to form the handle.

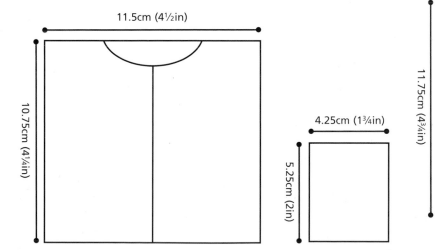

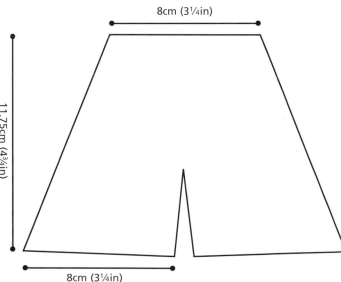

Newborn Baby Bear

This wonderful little bear is the perfect way to celebrate the birth of a new baby. With a beautifully detailed blanket and adorable jacket, Newborn Baby Bear is sure to become a family heirloom.

SKILL LEVEL
Advanced

MATERIALS
For the jacket and blanket
- 226m (246yd) DK weight yarn (A). The bear's outfit opposite uses two balls Rowan Wool Cotton, 50% wool, 50% cotton, 50g (1oz), 113m (123yd), 900 Antique

For the blanket
- 113m (123yd) DK weight yarn (B). The bear's outfit opposite uses one ball Rowan Wool Cotton, 50% wool, 50% cotton, 50g (1oz), 113m (123yd), 951 Tender
- 113m (123yd) DK weight yarn (C). The bear's outfit opposite uses one ball Rowan Wool Cotton, 50% wool, 50% cotton, 50g (1oz), 113m (123yd), 901 Citron
- 113m (123yd) DK weight yarn light (D). The bear's outfit opposite uses one ball Rowan Wool Cotton, 50% wool, 50% cotton, 50g (1oz), 113m (123yd), 941 Clear
- 113m (123yd) DK weight yarn (E). The bear's outfit opposite uses one ball Rowan Wool Cotton, 50% wool, 50% cotton, 50g (1oz), 113m (123yd), 952 Hiss
- 4mm (size 6) needles (or size needed to obtain tension)
- Large sewing needle

TENSION
22 stitches and 30 rows to 10cm (4in) using 4mm (size 6) needles and DK weight yarn, measured over stocking stitch.

JACKET
Back
Using 4mm (size 6) needles and A, cast on 33 stitches.
Row 1: K1, (p1, k1) to end.
Repeat row 1 27 more times, ending with a wrong-side row.
Row 29: Knit.
Repeat row 29 twice more. *
Row 32: P1, (p2tog, p2) to end. *25 stitches*
Row 33: Knit.
Row 34: Purl.
Repeat rows 33 and 34 four more times, ending with a wrong-side row.
Next row: K7, cast off centre 11 stitches, k7.
Do not cast off. Leave the two sets of shoulder stitches on a holder.

Right front
Using 4mm (size 6) needles and A, cast on 17 stitches.
Work as for Back until *.
Row 32: P1, (p2tog, p2) to end. *13 stitches*
Row 33: Knit.
Row 34: P12, k1.
Repeat rows 33 and 34 twice more.**
Row 39: Cast off 3 stitches, knit to end. *10 stitches*
Row 40: Purl to last 3 stitches, p2togtbl, k1. *9 stitches*
Row 41: K1, k2togtbl, knit to end. *8 stitches*
Row 42: Purl to last 3 stitches, p2togtbl, k1. *7 stitches*
Row 43: K7.
Do not cast off. Leave the shoulder stitches on a holder.

Left front
Work as for Right Front until **.
Row 39: Knit.
Row 40: Cast off 3 stitches, purl to end. *10 stitches*
Row 41: Knit to last 3 stitches, k2tog, k1. *9 stitches*
Row 42: K1, p2tog, purl to end. *8 stitches*
Row 43: Knit to last 3 stitches, k2tog, k1. *7 stitches*
Do not cast off. Leave the shoulder stitches on a holder.

SLEEVES (MAKE 2)
Using 4mm (size 6) needles and A, cast on 19 stitches.
Row 1: K1, (p1, k1) to end.
Repeat row 1 twice more.
Row 4: Purl.
Row 5: Knit.
Row 6: Purl.
Repeat rows 5 and 6 six more times, ending with a wrong-side row.
Cast off.

BLANKET
Front
Using the intarsia method and 4mm (size 6) needles, cast on as follows:
Cast on 9 stitches in B, 9 stitches in A, 9 stitches in C, 9 stitches in D, and 9 stitches in E. *45 stitches*
Work the next 72 rows from chart on page 72.
Cast off in seed stitch.

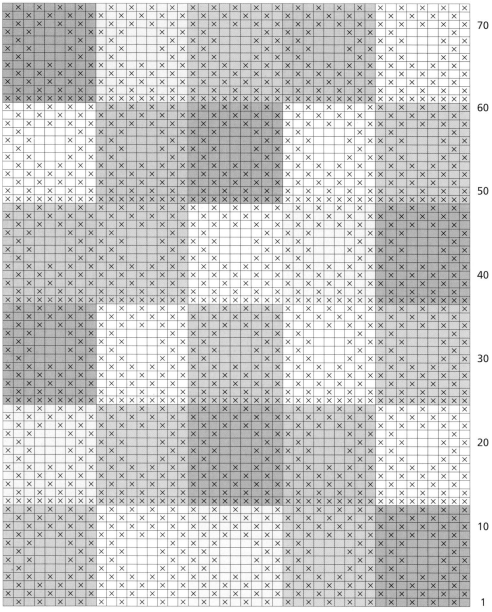

70

60

50

40

30

20

10

1

45 stitches

KEY:

☐   Knit on rs, Purl on ws

☒   Purl on rs, Knit on ws

  Complex Medium-Sized Bear

KEY:

⊠ Knit on rs, Purl on ws using contrasting shade

☐ Knit on rs, Purl on ws

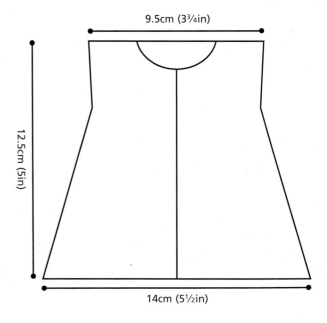

Back

Using 4mm (size 6) needles and A, cast on 45 stitches.

Row 1: K1, (p1, k1) to end.

Repeat row 1 nine more times, ending with a wrong-side row. Working seed stitch border as set by the first 10 rows, continue as follows:

Row 11: Work in seed stitch for 5 stitches, knit to last 5 stitches, work in seed stitch to end.

Row 12: Work in seed stitch for 5 stitches, purl to last 5 stitches, work in seed stitch to end.

Repeat rows 11 and 12 eight more times, ending with a wrong-side row.

Keeping seed stitch border correct as set, work the next 9 rows of the centre panel from the chart on page 73, inserting the letters of your choice in one of the contrasting shades.

Next row: Work in seed stitch for 5 stitches, purl to last 5 stitches, work in seed stitch to end.

Next row: Work in seed stitch for 5 stitches, knit to last 5 stitches, work in seed stitch to end.

Next row: Work in seed stitch for 5 stitches, purl to last 5 stitches, work in seed stitch to end.

Repeat last 2 rows seven more times, ending with a wrong-side row.

Next row: K1, (p1, k1) to end.

Repeat last row nine more times, ending with a wrong-side row.

Cast off in seed stitch.

FINISHING

JACKET

Join both shoulder seams using the three-needle cast-off technique as described on page 26.

Sleeves

Fold sleeve in half lengthwise and mark the centre of the cast-off edge with a stitch marker. Line up this marker with the shoulder seam and baste the sleeve in place. Now sew the sleeve to the body. Attach both sleeves in the same way.

Join both side and sleeve seams.

BLANKET

Stitch the front and back pieces together using A.

4.25cm (1¾in)

6cm (2¼in)

4cm (1½in)

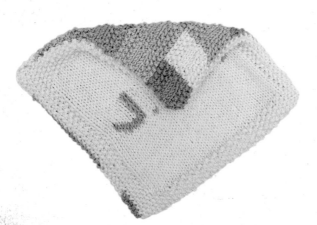

9.5cm (3¾in)

12.5cm (5in)

14cm (5½in)

Cowboy Bear

Cowboy Bear is all saddled up and ready for Wild West adventures. With his lasso, cowboy shirt and chaps, he's certain to become a favourite toy for kids of all ages.

SKILL LEVEL
Intermediate

MATERIALS

For the chaps
- 180m (197yd) sock weight yarn (A). The bear's outfit on this page uses one ball Rowan Classic Cashsoft 4ply, 57% extra fine merino, 33% microfibre, 10% cashmere, 50g (1oz), 197m (215yd), 441 Walnut

For the neck scarf
- 180m (197yd) sock weight yarn (B). The bear's outfit on this page uses one ball Rowan Classic Cashsoft 4ply, 429 Redwood

For the shirt
- 175m (191yd) sock weight yarn (C). The bear's outfit on this page uses one ball Rowan 4ply Soft, 100% Merino wool, 50g (1oz), 175m (191yd), 383 Black

For the jeans
- One ball Rowan Denim, 100% cotton, 50g (1oz), 93m (101yd), 229 Memphis (D)

For the shirt embroidery
- 115m (126yd) 4ply yarn (E). The bear's outfit on page 76 uses small amount Rowan Cotton Glace, 100% cotton, 50g (1oz), 115m (137yd), 726 Bleached
- 3.25mm and 4mm (sizes 3 and 6) needles (or size needed to obtain tension)
- Large sewing needle
- Approximately 1m (1yd) length of leather cord
- Five 7mm press fasteners

TENSION

JEANS

Before washing:

20 stitches and 28 rows to 10cm (4in) using
4mm (size 6) needles and Denim measured
over stocking stitch.

After washing:

20 stitches and 32 rows to 10cm (4in) using
4mm (size 6) needles and Denim measured
over stocking stitch.

CHAPS/SCARF

28 stitches and 36 rows to 10cm (4in) using
3.25mm (size 3) needles and sock weight yarn,
measured over stocking stitch.

SHIRT

28 stitches and 36 rows to 10cm (4in) using
3.25mm (size 3) needles and sock weight yarn,
measured over stocking stitch.

JEANS

Back

Leg (make 2)

Using 4mm (size 6) needles and D, cast on
15 stitches.

Row 1: Knit.

Row 2: Purl.

Repeat rows 1 and 2 until the work measures
15cm (6in) from cast-on edge.

Do not cast off. Leave the stitches on a holder.

Join the two legs of the back as follows:

With right sides facing, knit across the
15 stitches of the left leg, then the
15 stitches of the other leg. *30 stitches*

Row 1: P14, p2tog, purl to end. *29 stitches*

Row 2: K14, p1, k14.

Row 3: P14, k1, p14.

Repeat rows 2 and 3 three more times, ending
with a wrong-side row.

Row 10: K14, p1, k14.

Row 11: Knit.

Row 12: Knit.

Row 13: Purl.

Row 14: Purl.

Cast off.

Front

Leg (make 2)

Using 4mm (size 6) needles and D, cast on
15 stitches.

Row 1: Knit.

Row 2: Purl.

Repeat rows 1 and 2 until the work measures
15cm (6in) from cast-on edge.

Do not cast off. Leave the stitches on a
holder.

Join the two legs of the front as follows:

With right sides facing, knit across the
15 stitches of the left leg and the 15
stitches of the other leg. *30 stitches*

Row 1: P14, p2tog, purl to end.
29 stitches

Row 2: K14, p1, k14.

Row 3: P14, k1, p14.

Row 4: K1, k2togtbl, k11, p1, k11, k2tog, k1.
27 stitches

Row 5: K1, p2tog, p10, k1, p10, p2togtbl, k1.
25 stitches

Row 6: K1, k2togtbl, k9, p1, k9, k2tog, k1.
23 stitches

Row 7: K1, p2tog, p8, k1, p8, p2togtbl, k1.
21 stitches

Row 8: K1, k2togtbl, k7, p1, k7, k2tog, k1.
19 stitches

Row 9: K1, p2tog, p6, k1, p6, p2togtbl, k1.
17 stitches

Row 10: K8, p1, k8.

Do not cast off. Leave the 17 stitches on a
holder.

Pocket inserts (make 2)

Using 4mm (size 6) needles and D, cast on
6 stitches.

Row 1: Knit.

Row 2: Purl.

Repeat rows 1 and 2 four more times, ending
with a wrong-side row.

Do not cast off. Leave the stitches on a holder.

Join pocket inserts as follows:

With wrong sides facing, knit across 6 stitches
of the right pocket insert, knit across 16
stitches from the front section, and knit across
the 6 stitches of the left pocket insert.
28 stitches

Next row: Knit.

Next row: Purl.

Next row: Purl.

Cast off.

Patch pockets (make 2)

Using 4mm (size 6) needles and D, cast on
7 stitches.

Row 1: Purl.

Row 2: K1, p5, k1.
Row 3: Knit.
Row 4: K1, p5, k1.
Repeat rows 3 and 4 three more times, ending with a wrong-side row.
Cast off.

CHAPS (MAKE 2)

Using 3.25mm (size 3) needles and A, cast on 27 stitches.
Row 1: K13, sl1, knit to end.
Row 2: K1, purl to last stitch, k1.
Repeat rows 1 and 2 22 more times, ending with a wrong-side row.
Do not cast off. Leave the stitches on a holder.
Join both chaps as follows:
K13, sl1, k13 across right chap, turn, cast on 7 stitches, turn, k13, sl2, and k13 across left chap. *61 stitches*
Next row: Cast on 7 stitches, purl to end. *68 stitches*
Next row: Cast on 11 stitches, k24, sl1, k33, sl1, knit to end. *79 stitches*
Next row: Purl.
Next row: K35, sl1, k33, sl1, knit to end. *79 stitches*
Next row: Purl.
Cast off.

ANKLE STRAPS (MAKE 2)

Using 3.25mm (size 3) needles and A, work as follows:
Measure 1cm (⅝in) up the front opening of the right chap and pick up and knit 4 stitches. Work on these 4 stitches as follows:
Row 1: K1, p2, k1.
Row 2: Knit.
Row 3: K1, p2, k1.
Repeat rows 2 and 3 seven more times, ending with a wrong-side row.
Cast off.

SHIRT

Back

Using 3.25mm (size 3) needles and C, cast on 29 stitches.
Row 1 (RS): Purl.
Row 2: Knit.
Repeat rows 1 and 2 10 more times, ending with a wrong-side row.
Row 23: P14, k1, p14.
Row 24: K13, p3, k13.
Row 25: P12, k5, p12.
Row 26: K11, p7, k11.
Row 27: P10, k9, p10.
Row 28: K9, p11, k9.
Row 29: P7, k15, p7.
Row 30: K5, p19, k5.
Row 31: P4, k21, p4.
Row 32: K2, p25, k2.
Row 33: Knit.
Row 34: Purl.
Row 35: Knit.
Row 36: P8, cast off centre 13 stitches, p8.
Do not cast off. Leave the two sets of shoulder stitches on a holder.

Right front

Using 3.25mm (size 3) needles and C, cast on 16 stitches.
Row 1: Purl.
Row 2: Knit.
Repeat rows 1 and 2 10 more times, ending with a wrong-side row.
Row 23: K1, p15.
Row 24: K14, p2.
Row 25: K3, p13.
Row 26: K12, p4.
Row 27: K5, p11.
Row 28: K10, p6.
Row 29: K8, p8.
Row 30: K6, p10.
Row 31: K12, p4.
Row 32: K2, p14.
Row 33: Cast off 6 stitches, knit to end.
Row 34: Purl to last 2 stitches, p2tog.
Row 35: K2tog, knit to end.
Row 36: Purl.
Do not cast off. Leave the shoulder stitches on a holder.

Left front

Using 3.25mm (size 3) needles and C, cast on 16 stitches.
Row 1: Purl.
Row 2: Knit.
Repeat rows 1 and 2 10 more times, ending with a wrong-side row.
Row 23: P15, k1.
Row 24: P2, k14.
Row 25: P13, k3.
Row 26: P4, k12.
Row 27: P11, k5.
Row 28: P6, k10.
Row 29: P8, k8.
Row 30: P10, k6.
Row 31: P4, k12.
Row 32: Cast off 6 stitches, p8, k2.

Row 33: Knit to last 2 stitches, k2tog.
Row 34: P2tog, purl to end.
Row 35: Knit.
Row 36: Purl.
Join both shoulder seams using the three-needle cast-off technique (see page 26), then work the collar as follows: Using 3.25mm (size 3) needles and C, and with wrong-side facing, pick up and knit 8 stitches up the left of the neck, 14 stitches across the back, and 8 stitches down the right of the neck.
30 stitches
Row 1: Purl.
Row 2: Knit.
Repeat rows 1 and 2 three more times, ending with a wrong-side row.
Next row: Purl.
Cast off.

SLEEVES (MAKE 2)

Using 3.25mm (size 3) needles and C, cast on 22 stitches.
Row 1: Purl.
Row 2: Knit.
Repeat rows 1 and 2 12 more times, ending with a wrong-side row.
Cast off.

NECK SCARF

Using 3.25mm (size 3) needles and B, cast on 3 stitches.
Row 1: Purl.
Row 2: K1, m1, k1, m1, k1. *5 stitches*
Row 3: Purl.

Row 4: K1, m1, knit to last stitch, m1, k1.
7 stitches
Repeat rows 3 and 4 until there are 17 stitches.
Row 15: K2, (m1, k4 3 times, m1, k3) to end.
21 stitches
Row 16: Purl.
Row 17: Knit.
Row 18: Purl.
Row 19: K3, (m1, k3) to end. *27 stitches*
Row 20: Purl.
Row 21: K3, (m1, k3) to end. *35 stitches*
Row 22: Cast on 15 stitches, knit to end.
50 stitches
Row 23: Cast on 15 stitches, purl to end.
65 stitches
Cast off.

FINISHING
JEANS

As Rowan Denim shrinks in length when washed for the first time, the front and back sections of the jeans, and enough yarn to sew them up, must be washed following the instructions on the ball band before the jeans are sewn together. If substituting another yarn, this may not be the case. Be sure to read your yarn's care instructions.

Join both front and back sections of the jeans as follows: Sew the outer side seams. Start at the top (cast-off edge) and work down to the bottom (cast-on edge). Now join the inner leg seams. Starting at the cast-on edge of the right leg, work up to the top, and then work down

the corresponding seam of the left leg.

Slip stitch the pocket inserts into place on the inside of the jeans. Stitch the patch pockets to the outside of the back of the jeans at the top of each leg. Around the waistband, sew vertical straight stitches to form belt loops. Cut a length of yarn and thread this around the waistband, under the belt loops. This length of yarn can be pulled to fit the waist of the bear snugly.

SHIRT
Sleeves: Fold sleeve in half lengthwise and mark the centre of the cast-off edge with a stitch marker. Line up this marker with the shoulder seam and baste the sleeve in place. Now sew the sleeve to the body. Attach both sleeves in the same way. Join both side and sleeve seams.

Sew press fasteners to the front opening, positioning one just below the neck, one just above the cast-on edge, and the other in between.

CHAPS
Sew one half of a press fastener to the wrong side of each ankle strap at the cast-off edge. Using the photograph as a guide, stretch the strap around the leg and mark a suitable position for the corresponding half of the press fastener. Sew in place.

The right-hand side of the waistband is slightly longer than the left (where you cast on 11 stitches) and it's on this end that you are going to sew the final press fastener. Sew one half of the press fastener to the wrong side of this longer band and sew the corresponding half of the press fastener to the right side of the waistband so that the chaps fit snugly around the bear's waist, over the jeans.

Embroidery: The shirt has stocking stitch detailing across the shoulders (front and back) which is in contrast to the reverse stocking stitch of the main shirt. To highlight this further, use E and a large sewing needle to create a running stitch which forms a border around this detailing. In the same way, embroider a breast pocket on both the right and left fronts.

LASSO

The leather cord is to be used as Cowboy Bear's lasso. This can be worn as shown or coiled around and worn over his arm or shoulder.

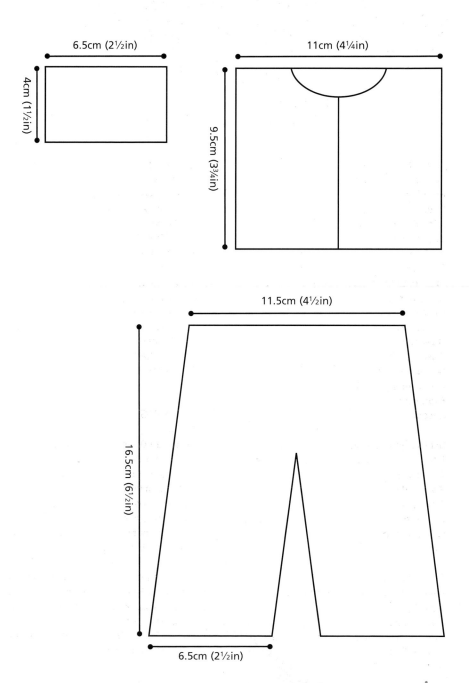

Complex Large Bear

With its two-tone colouring and jointed arms and legs, you can't help falling in love with this large teddy. This pattern is ideal for more advanced knitters and creates a truly adorable bear.

FINISHED SIZE
Height: 35cm (13¾in)
Diameter (around body): 30cm (11⅞in)

MATERIALS
Option A (Beige contrast)
- 175m (191yd) DK weight yarn used double throughout (A). The bear on page 87 uses two balls Rowan Felted Tweed, 50% Merino wool, 25% alpaca, 25% viscose/rayon, 50g (1oz), 175m (191yd), 157 Camel
- 130m (142yd) DK weight yarn (B). The bear on page 87 uses one ball Rowan Cashsoft DK, 57% extra fine merino, 33% microfibre, 10% cashmere, 50g (1oz), 130m (142yd), 507 Savannah

Option B (Cream contrast)
- 175m (191yd) DK weight yarn used double throughout (A). The bear on page 82 uses two balls Rowan Felted Tweed, 50% Merino wool, 25% alpaca, 25% viscose/rayon, 50g (1oz), 175m (191yd), 156 Wheat
- 130m (142yd) DK weight yarn (B). The bear on page 82 uses one ball Rowan Cashsoft DK, 57% extra fine merino, 33% microfibre, 10% cashmere, 50g (1oz), 130m (142yd), 500 Cream
- 4mm and 4.5mm (sizes 6 and 7) needles (or size needed to obtain tension)
- 160m (175yd) 4ply yarn for facial features. The bear on page 82 uses small amount Rowan Calmer, 75% cotton, 25% acrylic, 50g (1oz), 160m (175yd), 481 Coffee Bean

- Four white plastic 16mm (⅝in) teddy bear joints
- 85g (3oz) toy stuffing

TENSION
20 stitches and 30 rows to 10cm (4in) using 4mm (size 6) needles and DK weight yarn (used double) measured over stocking stitch.

BODY
Sides (make 2)
Using 4.5mm (size 7) needles and A (used double), cast on 9 stitches. Work as for knitting the body until * on page 62.
Repeat rows 18 and 19 10 more times ending with a right-side row.
Row 42: Knit.
Row 43: P9, p2tog, p1, p2togtbl, purl to end. *21 stitches*
Row 44: Knit.
Row 45: P8, p2tog, p1, p2togtbl, purl to end. *19 stitches*
Row 46: K7, k2togtbl, k1, k2tog, knit to end. *17 stitches*
Row 47: P6, p2tog, p1, p2togtbl, purl to end. *15 stitches*
Row 48: K5, k2togtbl, k1, k2tog, knit to end. *13 stitches*
Row 49: P4, p2tog, p1, p2togtbl, purl to end. *11 stitches*
Row 50: K3, k2togtbl, k1, k2tog, knit to end. *9 stitches*
Row 51: (P2tog) four times, k1. *5 stitches*
Do not cast off. Thread yarn through the remaining stitches, pull together and secure.

HEAD
Left side
Using 4mm (size 6) needles and A (used double), cast on 13 stitches. Work as for knitting the left side of the head on page 62.

Right side
Using 4mm (size 6) needles and A (used double), cast on 13 stitches. Work as for knitting the right side of the head on page 63.

Head gusset
Using 4mm (size 6) needles and A (used double), cast on 4 stitches. Work as for knitting the head gusset on page 63.

LEGS (MAKE 2)
Using 4mm (size 6) needles and A (used double), cast on 17 stitches. Work as for knitting the legs on page 63.

FEET PADS (MAKE 2)
Using 4mm (size 6) needles B, cast on 3 stitches. Work as for knitting the feet pads on page 64.

ARMS
Inner arms (make 2)
Using 4mm (size 6) needles and B, cast on 3 stitches. Work as for knitting the inner arms on page 64. **Remember to use yarn A doubled when changing yarns.**

Outer arms (make 2)
Using 4mm (size 6) needles and A (used double), cast on 3 stitches. Work as for knitting the outer arms on page 64.

Ears (make 2)

Using 4mm (size 6) needles and B, cast on 7 stitches.

Row 1: Knit.

Row 2: K1, p5, k1.

Repeat rows 1 and 2 once more.

Row 5: K2tog, knit to last 2 stitches, k2tog. *5 stitches*

Cast off and, **at the same time**, k2tog at each end of the cast-off row. Leave a long enough tail to shape ear and attach it to the head.

FINISHING

HEAD

Work as for finishing the head on page 64.

FACIAL FEATURES

Using the brown yarn (Rowan Calmer shade 481), sew the bear's facial features as follows:

Eyes

Work as for finishing the eyes on page 64.

Nose and mouth

Work as for finishing the nose and mouth on page 65.

BODY

Sew the two pieces together as follows (the seams are at the centre front and centre back of the body): Starting at the cast-on edge, sew the first seam all the way to the top of the body. Sew the other seam in the same way but stop approximately two-thirds of the way up. Join the cast-on edges of the two pieces. Using the opening that you have left, insert the shank half of the joints for the legs and arms. Use the shaping on the body as a guide. For the legs, position the joints approximately 1cm (³⁄₈in) up from the start of the side shaping, and for the arms, position the joints at the beginning of shoulder shaping.

Then stuff the body until it is firm and roughly 20cm (7¾in) in diameter (using the photograph as a guide to help you to achieve a good shape). Sew up the remaining third of the second seam. Fasten securely.

You may want to put some of the stuffing in before you position your joints so that you can see the shape better – do whatever works best for your bear.

ARMS

Each arm has an outer section and an inner section. The inner section has a paw pad in the contrasting yarn. Join the inner section to the outer section starting at the top of the arm, working down one side and then up the other, stopping approximately two-thirds of the way up. Position the arm so that the top of the inner section meets the shank of the shoulder joint (level with the shoulder). When you are happy with the positioning, push the shank through the knitted fabric and secure inside the arm with the washer half of the joint. Then, using the opening you have left, stuff the arm until it is firm, then sew up the remaining third of the seam. Fasten securely.

LEGS

Each leg has been knitted in one piece and will have a foot pad attached at the sole. Fold the leg in half lengthwise and sew the two cast-on edges together two-thirds of the way so that you leave an opening, forming a seam that runs down the back of the leg. When folding the length in half, you will have folded the cast-on edge in half too. Join these two edges together, creating a seam that runs across the top of the leg from front to back. Position the leg so that the top of the inside leg meets up with the shank of the leg joint. When you are happy with the positioning, push the shank through the knitted fabric and secure inside the leg with the washer half of the joint. Now firmly stuff the leg and sew up the opening, then attach the foot pad by sewing around the edges of the pad, joining it to the cast-off edge of the leg.

Ears

Work as for finishing the ears on page 65.

ASSEMBLING YOUR BEAR

Your bear's arms and legs have been attached with joints, and so all that remains is to attach the head. Sew the head securely to the top centre top of the body.

First Birthday Bear

Celebrate an important milestone with First Birthday Bear. Dressed in pink for a girl or blue for a boy, and complete with a little birthday cupcake, this bear is sure to bring a touch of magic to your little one's special day.

SKILL LEVEL
Intermediate

MATERIALS

For the sweater
Boy's version
- 170m (186yd) aran weight yarn (A). The bear's outfit opposite uses two balls Rowan Handknit Cotton, 100% cotton, 50g (1oz), 85m (93yd), 327 Aqua

Girl's version
- 170m(186yd) aran weight yarn (B). The bear's outfit opposite uses two balls Rowan Handknit Cotton, 332 Rose

For the hat trim
- 170m (186yd) aran weight yarn (C). The bear's outfit opposite uses one ball Rowan Handknit Cotton, 263 Bleached
- Approximately 1m (40in) silver curling ribbon
- 40.5cm (16in) white elastic

Boy and Girl
- 2.75mm, 3.25mm, 3.75mm, and 4mm (sizes 2, 3, 5, and 6) needles (or size needed to obtain tension)
- Large sewing needle
- Sewing thread

For the cupcake
- 115m (126yd) 4ply yarn (D). The cake on page 85 uses one ball Rowan Cotton Glace, 100% cotton, 50g (1oz), 115m (137yd), 725 Ecru
- 113m (123yd) DK weight yarn (E). The cake on page 85 uses one ball Rowan Wool Cotton, 50% wool, 50% cotton, 50g (1oz), 113m(123yd), 929 Dream

- Small amount of aran weight yarn (F). The cupcakes on page 85 use small amounts of Rowan Handknit Cotton, 327 Aqua and 310 Shell, for icing
- Small amount of 4ply yarn. The cupcake on page 85 use small amounts Rowan Cotton Glace shades 726 Bleached (G) and 833 Ochre (H), for candle
- Approximately 23 3mm white beads, such as Rowan 01016 for cupcake with beads
- 3.25mm (size 3) double-pointed needles (or size needed to obtain tension)
- Small amount of toy stuffing

TENSION
20 stitches and 28 rows to 10cm (4in) using 4mm (size 6) needles and aran weight yarn, measured over stocking stitch.

SWEATER

Back
Using 3.25mm (size 3) needles and A for boy's version or B for girl's version, cast on 33 stitches.
Row 1: K1, (p1, k1) to end.
Repeat row 1 three more times, ending with a wrong-side row.
Change to 4mm (size 6) needles
Row 5: Knit.
Row 6: Purl.
Repeat rows 5 and 6 14 more times, ending with a wrong-side row.
Next row: K6, cast off centre 21 stitches, k6.
Do not cast off. Leave both sets of shoulder stitches on holders.

Front
Using 3.25mm (size 3) needles and A for boy's version or B for girl's version, cast on 33 stitches.
Row 1: K1, (p1, k1) to end.
Repeat row 1 three more times, ending with a wrong-side row.
Change to 4mm (size 6) needles
Row 5: Knit.
Row 6: Purl.
Repeat rows rows 5 and 6 10 more times, ending with a wrong-side row.
Row 27: K12, turn and work on these 12 stitches only as follows:
Row 28: Purl.
Row 29: Knit to last 3 stitches, k2tog, k1. *11 stitches*
Row 30: P1, p2tog, purl to end. *10 stitches*
Repeat rows 29 and 30 until 6 stitches remain.
Row 35: Knit.
Row 36: Purl.
Do not cast off. Leave the shoulder stitches on a holder.
With right side facing, rejoin yarn to remaining stitches and work as follows:
Next row: Cast off centre 9 stitches, knit to end.
Row 28: Purl.
Row 29: K1, k2togtbl, knit to end. *11 stitches*
Row 30: Purl to last 3 stitches, p2togtbl, p1. *10 stitches*
Repeat rows 29 and 30 until 6 stitches remain.
Row 35: Knit.
Row 36: Purl.
Do not cast off. Leave the shoulder stitches on a holder.

NECKBAND

Join the right shoulder using the three-needle cast-off technique as described on page 26. With right side facing, using 4mm (size 6) needles and A for boy's version or B for girl's version, pick up and knit 10 stitches down the left front of the neck, 9 stitches across the centre front, 10 stitches up the right front of the neck, and 22 stitches across the back. *51 stitches*

Row 1: K1, (p1, k1) to end.
Repeat row 1 once more.
Cast off in seed stitch.

Sleeves (make 2)

Using 3.25mm (size 3) needles and A for boy's version or B for girl's version, cast on 25 stitches.

Row 1: K1, (p1, k1) to end
Repeat row 1 three more times, ending with a wrong-side row.

Change to 4mm (size 6) needles.
Row 5: Knit.
Row 6: Purl.
Repeat rows 5 and 6 three more times, ending with a wrong-side row.
Cast off.

PARTY HAT

Using 3.25mm (size 3) needles and C, cast on 29 stitches.
Row 1: Knit.
Row 2: Knit.
Change to 4mm (size 6) needles and A for boy's version or B for girl's version.
Row 3: Knit.
Row 4: Purl.
Row 5: Knit.
Row 6: Purl.
Row 7: K2tog, knit to last 2 stitches, k2tog. *27 stitches*
Row 8: Purl.

Repeat rows 7 and 8 until 19 stitches remain, ending with a wrong-side row.
Next row: K2tog, knit to last 2 stitches, k2tog.
Next row: P2tog, purl to last 2 stitches, p2tog.
Repeat last 2 rows until 3 stitches remain.
Next row: K3tog.
Fasten off.

CUPCAKE

Cupcake case – side

Using 4mm (size 6) needles and D, cast on 42 stitches.
Row 1: K2, (p1, k1) to last 2 stitches, p2.
Repeat row 1 once more.
Change to 3.25mm (size 3) needles.
Repeat row 1 six more times, ending with a wrong-side row.
Change to 2.75mm (size 2) needles.
Repeat row 1 until work measures 5cm (2in) from cast-on edge, ending with a wrong-side row.
Cast off.

Cupcake case – base

Using 2.75mm (size 2) needles and D, cast on 5 stitches.
Row 1: Purl.
Row 2: K1, m1, k3, m1, k1. *7 stitches*
Row 3: Purl.
Row 4: K1, m1, k5, m1, k1. *9 stitches*
Row 5: Purl.
Row 6: K1, m1, k7, m1, k1. *11 stitches*
Row 7: Purl.
Row 8: Knit.
Row 9: Purl.
Row 10: K2togtbl, k7, k2togtbl. *9 stitches*
Row 11: Purl.
Row 12: K2togtbl, k5, k2togtbl. *7 stitches*
Row 13: Purl.
Row 14: K2togtbl, k3, k2togtbl. *5 stitches*
Row 15: Purl.
Cast off.

Cupcake

Using 3.75mm (size 5) needles and E, cast on 10 stitches.
Row 1: Purl.
Row 2: K2, m1, k1, m1, k1, m1, k2, m1, k1, m1, k1, m1, k2. *16 stitches*
Row 3: Purl.
Row 4: Knit.
Row 5: Purl.
Row 6: K1, (m1, k2) to last stitch, m1, k1. *24 stitches*
Row 7: Purl.
Row 8: Knit.
Repeat rows 7 and 8 four more times, and then row 7 once more.
Row 18: K2tog, (k1, k2tog) to last 2 stitches, k2. *17 stitches*
Row 19: Purl.
Row 20: Knit.
Row 21: Purl.
Row 22: K2tog, k2, (k2tog) to last stitch, k1. *10 stitches*
Row 23: Purl.
Cast off.

Icing

Using 2.75mm (size 2) needles and F (in the shade of your choice) cast on 5 stitches.
Row 1: K1, p3, k1.
Row 2: K1, m1, k3, m1, k1. *7 stitches*
Row 3: K1, p5, k1.
Row 4: K1, m1, k5, m1, k1. *9 stitches*
Row 5: K1, p7, k1.
Row 6: K1, m1, k7, m1, k1. *11 stitches*
Row 7: K1, p9, k1.
Row 8: Knit.
Row 9: K1, p9, k1.
Row 10: K2togtbl, k7, k2togtbl. *9 stitches*
Row 11: K1, p7, k1.
Row 12: K2togtbl, k5, k2togtbl. *7 stitches*
Row 13: K1, p5, k1.
Row 14: K2togtbl, k3, k2togtbl. *5 stitches*

Row 15: K1, p3, k1.
Cast off.

Candle

Using the technique described below, make the candle from an I-cord as follows:
Using 3.25mm (size 3) double-pointed needles and G, cast on 3 stitches
Row 1: Knit.
Repeat row 1 until cord is 4cm (1⅝in).
Break off yarn, thread through remaining stitches and pull together.

Technique for making I-cord: Once you have cast on your stitches, knit one row. You would now usually turn your needles but to make the cord, do not turn. Instead, slide the stitches to the other end of the double-pointed needle, ready to be knitted again. The yarn will now be at the left edge of the knitting and so, to knit, you must pull it tightly across the back of your work and then knit one row. You continue in this way, never turning and always sliding the work to the other end of the double-pointed needle, and the right side of the work will always be facing you.

Flame

Using 3.25mm (size 3) needles and H, cast on 3 stitches.
Row 1: K1, p1, k1.
Row 2: K1, m1, k1, m1, k1. *5 stitches*
Row 3: K1, p3, k1.
Row 4: K1, sl2, k1, p2sso, k1. *3 stitches*
Row 5: Sl2, k1, p2sso. *1 stitch*
Fasten off, leaving a long tail.

FINISHING
SWEATER

Join the left shoulder seam using the three-needle cast-off technique as described on page 26.

Sleeves

Fold sleeve in half lengthwise and mark the centre of the cast-off edge with a stitch marker. Line up this marker with the shoulder seam and baste the sleeve in place. Now sew the sleeve to the body. Attach both sleeves in the same way.
Join both side and sleeve seams.

PARTY HAT

Sew the side seams together by starting at the cast-on edge and working up to the point of the hat, creating a seam at the back.

Using the photograph as a guide, embroider a number 1 using Swiss darning on the centre front of the hat. Attach two 25cm (10in) lengths of curling ribbon to the point of the hat.

Sew each end of an 20.5cm (8in) length of white elastic to each side of the hat, inside the cast-on edge.

CUPCAKE

Sew together the two side seams of the cupcake case. Join the sides of the case to the base by stitching the edge of the base to the cast-off edge of the sides. Fill the holder with stuffing and then insert the cupcake onto the top of this so that the edges of the cake sit just inside the top of the case. You may want to put a bit more stuffing in or take a bit out, depending on the shape. When you are happy with the shape of the cupcake, slip stitch the edges of the cupcake inside the rim of the case. Stitch the icing to the top of the cupcake.

Cupcake with candle

Thread the long tail that was left after fastening off the flame onto a sewing needle. Stitch the flame to the top of the candle and then thread the yarn down through the centre of the knitted I-cord and out through the bottom. Stitch the base of the candle to the top of the cake.

Cupcake with white beads

Using a fine sewing needle and thread, stitch the beads in a random fashion to the top of the icing.

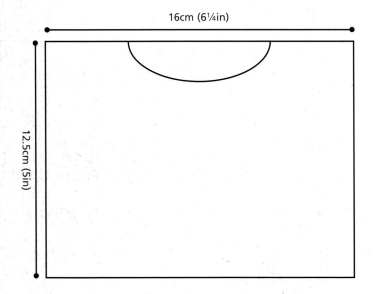

16cm (6¼in)

12.5cm (5in)

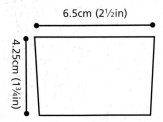

6.5cm (2½in)

4.25cm (1¾in)

SKILL LEVEL
Simple

MATERIALS
For the bikini
- 113m (123yd) DK weight yarn. The bear's outfit on this page uses one ball Rowan Wool Cotton, 50% wool, 50% cotton, 50g (1oz), 113m (123yd), 943 Flower
- 4mm (size 6) needles (or size needed to obtain tension)
- Six 8mm pink beads
- One 7mm press fastener
- Large sewing needle

TENSION
22 stitches and 30 rows to 10cm (4in) using 4mm (size 6) needles and DK weight yarn, measured over stocking stitch.

BIKINI TOP (MAKE 2)
Using 4mm (size 6) needles, cast on 15 stitches.
Row 1: Purl.
Repeat row 1 once more.
Row 3: K2, yo, k2tog, (k1, yo, k2tog) to last 2 stitches, k2.
Row 4: Knit.
Row 5: Knit.
Row 6: K1, purl to last stitch, k1.
Row 7: K1, k2togtbl, knit to last 3 stitches, k2tog, k1. *13 stitches*
Repeat rows 6 and 7 until 5 stitches remain.
Next row: K1, p3, k1.
Next row: K1, sl2, k1, p2sso, k1. *3 stitches*
Next row: K1, p1, k1.
Next row: Knit.

Swimmer Bear

In her adorable little bikini, Swimmer Bear is all ready to soak up the sun on holiday.

Repeat last 2 rows until work measures 13cm (5⅛in) from cast-on edge.
Cast off.

BIKINI BOTTOMS (MAKE 2)
Using 4mm (size 6) needles, cast on 27 stitches.
Row 1: Purl.
Row 2: Purl.
Row 3: K2, yo, k2tog, (k1, yo, k2tog) to last 2 stitches, k2.
Row 4: Knit.
Row 5: Knit.
Row 6: K1, purl to last stitch, k1.
Row 7: K1, k2togtbl, knit to last 3 stitches, k2tog, k1. *25 stitches*
Repeat rows 6 and 7 until 19 stitches remain.
Next row: K1, p2tog, purl to last 3 stitches, k2tog, k1. *17 stitches*
Next row: K1, k2togtbl, knit to last 3 stitches, k2tog, k1. *15 stitches*
Repeat last 2 rows until 7 stitches remain.
Next row: K1, purl to last stitch, k1.
Next row: Knit.
Next row: K1, purl to last stitch, k1.
Do not cast off. Leave the stitches on a holder.

FINISHING
BIKINI TOP
Sew one half of the press fastener to the wrong side of the cast-off end of the left strap, and the other half of the press fastener to the right side of the cast-off end of the right strap.

BIKINI BOTTOMS
Join the two halves of the bikini bottoms using the three-needle cast-off technique as described on page 26.
Make twisted cords as follows:

Medium length (make 2)
Cut two strands of yarn approximately 125cm (50in) in length. Take the strands of yarn and secure at each end with knots. Ask someone to help you and give them one end of the yarn while you hold the other. With the yarn outstretched, twist each end in opposite directions until it shows signs of twisting back on itself. Bring the two ends of the cord together and hold tightly, allowing the two halves to twist together. Smooth out any bumps by running your fingers up and down the cord. You will now have a twisted cord measuring approximately 50cm (20in).

Longer length (make 1)
Work as for the medium length cord but start with strands measuring approiximately 175cm (70in). You will end with a cord that is approximately 70cm (27½in).

Thread a bead onto each end of the three cords and secure with a knot.

Thread the longer cord through the eyelets of each section of the bikini top and tie at the back.

Thread one of the medium lengths of cord through the eyelets of one of the sections of the bikini bottoms, then the other cord through the other section. Cords will tie at the sides.

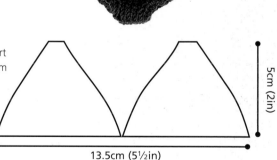

5cm (2in)

13.5cm (5½in)

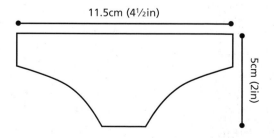

11.5cm (4½in)

5cm (2in)

Golfer Bear

Perfect for sports fans, Golfer Bear is all dressed and ready to tee off. His smart Fair Isle sweater will be the envy of everyone on the green!

SKILL LEVEL
Advanced

MATERIALS
For the tank top
- 110m (120yd) 4ply yarn (A). The bear's outfit opposite uses one ball Rowan Scottish Tweed 4ply, 100% wool, 50g (1oz), 110m (120yd), 025 Oatmeal
- 175m (191yd) 4ply yarn (B). The bear's outfit opposite uses one ball Rowan 4 ply Soft, 100% Merino wool, 50g (1oz), 175m (191yd), 372 Sooty
- 110m (120yd) sock weight yarn (C). The bear's outfit opposite uses one ball Rowan Scottish Tweed 4ply, 015 Apple

For the tank top and visor
- 110m (120yd) sock weight yarn (D). The bear's outfit opposite uses one ball Rowan Scottish Tweed 4ply, 017 Lobster
- 180m (197yd) sock weight yarn (E). The bear's outfit opposite uses one ball Rowan Classic Cashsoft 4ply, 57% extra fine merino, 33% microfibre, 10% cashmere, 50g (1oz), 197m (215yd), 433 Cream

For the trousers
- 113m (123yd) sock weight yarn (F). The bear's outfit opposite uses one ball Rowan Wool Cotton, 50% wool, 50% cotton, 50g (1¾oz), 113m (123yd), 963 Smalt

- 3.25mm and 4mm (sizes 3 and 6) needles (or size needed to obtain tension)
- One 7mm press fastener
- Large sewing needle

TENSION
TROUSERS
22 stitches and 30 rows to 10cm (4in) using 4mm (size 6) needles and 4ply yarn, measured over stocking stitch.

TANK TOP
28 stitches and 36 rows to 10cm (4in) using 3.25mm (size 3) needles and 4ply yarn, measured over stocking stitch.

TROUSERS
Front
Leg (make 2)
Using 3.25mm (size 3) needles and F, cast on 17 stitches.
Row 1: K1, (p1, k1) to end.
Row 2: P1, (k1, p1) to end.
Repeat rows 1 and 2 once more.
Change to 4mm (size 6) needles.
Row 5: K1, m1, (k5, m1) 3 times, k1. *21 stitches*
Row 6: Purl.
Row 7: Knit.
Row 8: Purl.
Repeat rows 7 and 8 eight more times. Do not cast off. Leave the stitches on a holder.
Join the two legs of the front section as follows:

With right sides facing and using 3.25mm (size 3) needles, knit across 20 stitches of the left leg, knit the last stitch of the left leg together with the first stitch of the right leg, knit to end. *41 stitches*
Row 1: Purl.
Row 2: K5, k2tog, (k3, k2tog) to last 4 stitches, k4. *34 stitches*
Row 3: Purl.
Row 4: Knit.
Row 5: Purl.
Repeat rows 4 and 5 seven more times, ending with a right-side row.
Next row: (K1, p1) to end.
Repeat last row three more times, ending with a wrong-side row.
Cast off in rib pattern.

Back section
Work as for the Front.

TANK TOP

Front

Using 3.25mm (size 3) needles and E, cast on 48 stitches.

Row 1: (K1, p1) to end.

Repeat row 1 three more times, ending with a wrong-side row.

Starting with a right-side row, work the next 28 rows from the chart on page 90.

Next, working in A only, continue as follows:

Next row: Cast off 6 stitches, k18, turn and work on these 18 stitches only as follows:

Next row: Cast off 1 stitch, purl to end. *17 stitches*

Next row: Knit to last 3 stitches, k2tog, k1. *16 stitches*

Next row: K1, p2tog, purl to end. *15 stitches*

Repeat last 2 rows until 7 stitches remain.

Cast off.

Rejoin yarn to remaining stitches and work as follows:

Next row: Cast off 1 stitch, knit to end.

Next row: Cast off 6 stitches, purl to last 3 stitches, p2togtbl, k1end. *17 stitches*

Next row: K1, k2togtbl, knit to end. *16 stitches*

Next row: Purl to last 3 stitchess, p2togtbl, k1. *15 stitches*

Repeat last 2 rows until 7 stitches remain.

Do not cast off. Leave these shoulder stitches on a holder.

Back

Using 3.25mm (size 3) needles and E, cast on 48 stitches.

Row 1: (K1, p1) to end.

Repeat row 1 three more times, ending with a wrong-side row.

Change to yarn A.

Row 5: Knit.

Row 6: Purl.

Repeat rows 5 and 6 13 more times, ending with a wrong-side row.

Row 33: Cast off 6 stitches, knit to end. *42 stitches*

Row 34: Cast off 6 stitches, purl to end. *36 stitches*

Row 35: Knit.

Row 36: Purl.

Repeat rows 35 and 36 four more times, ending with a wrong-side row.

Row 41: K7, cast off centre 22 stitches, k7.

Slip the first set of 7 stitches (right shoulder) onto a holder and work on the second set of 7 stitches (left shoulder) as follows:

Next row: Purl.

Next row: Knit.

Repeat the last 2 rows once more, ending with a wrong-side row.

Cast off.

NECKBAND

Join the right shoulder using the three-needle cast-off technique as described on page 26. With right sides facing, using 3.25mm (size 3) needles and E, pick up and knit 12 stitches down the left front of the neck, 12 stitches up the right front of the neck, and 24 stitches across the back. *48 stitches*

Row 1: (K1, p1) to end.

Cast off loosely in rib pattern.

VISOR

Peak

Using 4mm (size 6) needles and D (with the yarn doubled), cast on 7 stitches.

Row 1: Purl.

Row 2: K1, (m1, k1) to end. *13 stitches*

Row 3: Purl.

Row 4: K1, (m1, k1) to end. *25 stitches*

Row 5: Purl.

Row 6: Knit.

Row 7: Purl.

Row 8: K5, (m1, k5) to end. *29 stitches*

Row 9: Purl.

Row 10: Knit.

Row 11: Purl.

Cast off.

Headband

Using 4mm (size 6) needles and E (with the yarn doubled), pick up and knit 9 stitches along the right edge of the peak, 4 stitches along the centre (the curve), and 9 stitches along the left edge of the peak. *22 stitches*

Work as follows:

Next row: Cast on 18 stitches, purl to end.

Next row: Cast on 18 stitches, k40, wrap next

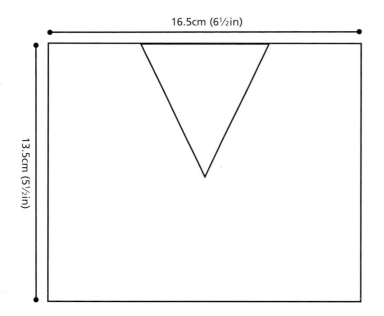

16.5cm (6½in)

13.5cm (5½in)

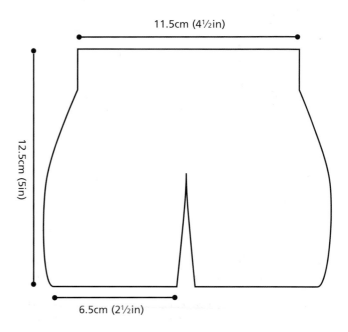

11.5cm (4½in)

12.5cm (5in)

6.5cm (2½in)

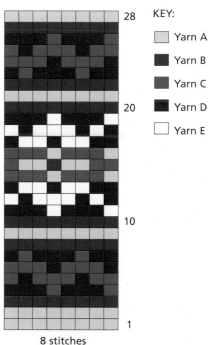

28

20

10

1

8 stitches

KEY:

Yarn A

Yarn B

Yarn C

Yarn D

Yarn E

stitch and turn.
Next row: P22, wrap next stitch and turn.
Next row: Knit to end.
Cast off.

FINISHING
TROUSERS
Join both the front and back sections of the
trousers as follows: Sew the outer side seams.
Start at the top (cast-off edge) and work down
to the bottom (cast-on edge). Now join the
inner leg seams. Starting at the cast-on edge of
the right leg, work up to the top, and then work
down the corresponding seam of the left leg.

TANK TOP
The left shoulder has been left open to make it
easier to pull off and on over the bear's head.
Sew one half of the press fastener to the right
side of the back shoulder, and the other half to
the wrong side of the front shoulder and
fasten.
Armhole edgings: Using 3.25mm (size 3)
needles and E, pick up and knit 34 stitches
around armhole edge. Cast off loosely.
Note: Take extra care when picking up the left
armhole band as the shoulder is only joined by
the press fastener. Make sure the front
shoulder is overlapping the back as you pick up.

YARN AND TENSION

QUANTITIES OF YARN AND DYE LOTS

At the beginning of each project the quantities of yarn are given. If different yarns are used, these quantities may alter. This is because the length of a ball of yarn depends on its weight and fibre content. If you are substituting yarns, you must check for the following things:

Check the tension of your preferred yarn against the tension of the pattern (the tension of the yarn can be found on the ball band and the tension of the pattern can be found at the beginning of the instructions). These must be the same if the substitution is to be successful.

Check the length of a ball of your preferred yarn against the length of a ball of the recommended yarn. The reason for this is that the weight of a ball of yarn varies between types. Therefore, you cannot rely on the weight to give you the correct amount of yarn – you must compare length.

If more than one ball of a particular colour is needed (for the basic bears, for example), ensure that you buy them from the same dye lot. The color of a specific shade of yarn can vary between dye lots and the change will show in the finished project.

TENSION

Tension can differ quite dramatically between knitters. This is because of the way that the needles and yarn are held. If your tension does not match that stated in the pattern, you should change your needle size following this simple rule:

If your knitting is too loose (fewer stitches and rows than the tension stated), you must use a smaller needle to make your knitting tighter. If your knitting is too tight (more stitches and rows than the tension stated), you must use a bigger needle to make your knitting looser. It is important that your tension is correct to ensure that the outfits fit your bear.

ABBREVIATIONS

PB Place bead: bring the yarn forward, slip bead to front of work, slip 1 st purlwise, take yarn to back of work. Bead will now be sitting in front of the slipped stitch.

P2B Place two beads: bring the yarn forward, slip two beads to front of work, slip 1 st purlwise, take yarn to back of work. Beads will now be sitting in front of the slipped stitch.

PS Place sequin: bring the yarn forward, slip sequin to front of work, slip 1 st purlwise, take yarn to back of work. Sequin will now be sitting in front of the slipped stitch.

ML Place sequin on a loop: knit into the next stitch and, before slipping the stitch off the left needle, slide a sequin up to the needle and bring the yarn to the front of the work between the needle points. Wrap the yarn around your left thumb and take it back between the needle points. Now, knit into the stitch again and then slip the stitch off the needle. You will now have two stitches on the right-hand needle. Cast one off by lifting one stitch over the other.

C6B Cable six back: Slip the next 3 stitches onto cable needle and hold at back of work, k3 from left needle and then knit the 3sts from the cable needle.

wrap st Wrap stitch: Slip the next stitch from the left to the right needle, bring the yarn forward between the needle points, slip the slipped stitch back onto the left needle and take the yarn to the back again.

k	knit
p	purl
rs	right side
ws	wrong side
k2tog	knit two stitches together
p2tog	purl two stitches together
k3tog	knit three stitches together
p3tog	purl three stitches together
k2togtbl	knit two stitches together through back of loop
p2togtbl	purl two stitches together through back of loop
m1	make one stitch
yo	yarn over
ybk	yarn back
yfwd	yarn forward
sl1	slip one stitch
sl2	slip two stitches
p2sso	pass two slipped stitches over

Intarsia Intarsia knitting produces a single thickness fabric that uses different balls of yarn for different areas of colour. There should be very little, if any, carrying across of yarns at the back of the work.

There are several ways to keep the separate colours of yarn organized when working in intarsia. My preferred method is to use yarn bobbins. Small amounts of yarn can be wound onto bobbins, which should then be kept close to the back of the work while knitting, and unwound only when more yarn is needed.

RESOURCES

Rowan yarns are widely distributed. To find a supplier near you, contact Rowan Yarns (see below) or visit the Rowan website.

Rowan Yarns
Green Lane Mill
Holmfirth
West Yorkshire
HD9 2DX

Tel: +44 (0)1484 681881
www.knitrowan.com

ACKNOWLEDGMENTS

A huge thank you to the following people who have all helped to make this book happen:

As always, thank you to Rowan for their wonderful yarns and to Kate Buller for allowing me to use these yarns to bring the teddies to life! To Sharon Brant whose support and invaluable advice I'd be lost without. To the team at Collins & Brown and in particular Miriam Hyslop for her help and guidance. To Sarah and Margaret for their kind words and help with the knitting. Lastly, a big thank you to Jez whose love and support as always was unwavering.

PICTURE CREDITS

Photography by Rachel Whiting
Front cover photography by Mark Winwood
Illustrations by Kang Chen